# LET GLOW-My New Mantra

# TABLE OF CONTENT

# I AM SHE

I am she
That girl who I tell other girls they should be
And that is free...
I've analyzed
Empathized
Then released the pain I held inside me
I'm no longer a prisoner to my body
So, I'm no longer looking for a better home than me
I am she
The girl who keeps bouncing back
Evening if the fall goes ways deep.
....
I've also stopped holding people's opinion to my chest
As if they were my own
"But thanks for your thoughts though..."
I am she
The girl who gets up, and keeps showing up no matter who sees
She, is me
And I am more than pleased with what is see
I'm not perfect
But those imperfections make me, me
So yes
I AM FREE!

-Gia N. Fraser

# INTRODUCTION

Self-love and self-acceptance are two concepts that are frequently discussed but not always fully comprehended. At their essence, they involve embracing our true selves, including our strengths and weaknesses, and treating ourselves with kindness, compassion, and respect. While these concepts may seem straightforward in theory, the path to achieving self-love and self-acceptance can be intricate and arduous. We often find ourselves influenced by societal expectations, personal insecurities, and negative self-talk, which can impede our ability to fully embrace and accept who we are. Nonetheless, the rewards of cultivating self-love and self-acceptance are profound, leading to improved self-esteem, stronger relationships with others, and a greater sense of fulfillment in life.

Within this book, we will embark on a journey exploring the path to self-love and self-acceptance. We will examine obstacles we may encounter along the way and delve into the benefits of wholeheartedly embracing ourselves, flaws, and all.

The journey towards self-discovery and self-actualization can be challenging yet rewarding. It demands that we confront our fears, expand our limited belief, and break free from negative patterns to construct a life that aligns with our values and aspirations. The process of personal growth and development is perpetual, requiring ongoing effort and dedication. In this guide, we will explore a multitude of strategies and techniques for personal growth and development. From nurturing self-love and self-compassion to embracing change and letting go of what no longer serves us, each step plays a vital role in our pursuit of becoming the best version of ourselves. By implementing these strategies, we can fashion a life that is purposeful, fulfilling, and in harmony with our authentic selves. Let us continue to grow, learn, and evolve as we navigate the journey of life through the pages of this book.

# CHAPTER 1

## Self-love and
## Self-acceptance

Self-love, it is a beautiful act of treating yourself with utmost kindness, compassion, and respect. It is about acknowledging your worth and realizing that you deserve nothing less than happiness and well-being. I have come to learn that self-love is not about striving for perfection; it is about embracing my authentic self, flaws, and all.

Self-acceptance plays a significant role, it is about wholeheartedly embracing every aspect of who you are, even the parts that aren't picture-perfect. It is understanding that nobody is flawless, and that is what makes us beautifully human. Lately, I've come to accept that my weaknesses and imperfections are an integral part of my being.

Furthermore, self-acceptance doesn't mean that you are completely satisfied with every little thing about yourself. It is more about recognizing your limitations and collaborating with them, while still valuing and loving yourself unconditionally. It is about embracing the whole package, appreciating my strengths and accept my weaknesses as opportunities for growth.

Together, self-love and self-acceptance have transformed my relationship with myself. They have taught me to be gentle with my soul, to be understanding when I stumble, and to celebrate my victories, no matter how small. It is an ongoing journey, one that requires patience and self-compassion. However, it is worth every step, because through self-love and self-acceptance, I've discovered a profound sense of inner-peace and a love for myself that knows no bounds.

## Obstacles in Seeking Self-love and Self-acceptance

Let us explore some of the obstacles we may encounter on our path to self-love and self-acceptance. It is important to acknowledge these challenges so that we can navigate through them with compassion and understanding.

One significant hurdle is the influence of societal expectations. Society often presents us with a narrow and unrealistic definition of beauty, success, and worthiness. It can make us feel inadequate and doubtful about ourselves. We might find ourselves striving for unattainable ideals, constantly comparing ourselves to others and feeling like we fall short. It is crucial to recognize that these expectations are subjective and do not define our true worth.

Another hurdle is cultural norms and traditions. These can play a role in obstructing self-love and self-acceptance. They impose stereotypes and expectations that may not align with our own values and beliefs. It can be challenging to navigate these conflicting messages and find the courage to embrace our authentic selves. Remember, our unique identity and individuality are to be celebrated, regardless of societal or cultural pressures.

Another obstacle we often face is personal insecurities and negative self-talk. Past experiences, such as the trauma or rejection, can leave deep imprints on our self-perception. They may lead us to doubt our abilities and worth, creating a constant inner dialogue promoting self-criticism. Additionally, comparing our-selves to others and seeking validation externally can perpetuate negative self-talk. It is important to cultivate self-compassion and challenge those negative thoughts by acknowledging our strengths and focusing on our personal growth.

The fear of rejection or receiving criticism can be a significant barrier to expressing self-love and self-acceptance. The fear of being judged or criticized may cause us to hide or suppress aspects of ourselves, preventing us from fully expressing who we are. Negative feedback or criticism can reinforce negative self-talk, intensifying self-doubt and impacting self-esteem. Remember, your self-worth is not determined by the opinions of others. Embracing vulnerability and surrounding ourselves with supportive and understanding individuals can help us overcome this fear.

Recognizing these obstacles is the first step towards overcoming them. Remember to be patient and gentle with yourself as you navigate these challenges. Embrace your journey towards self-love and self-acceptance, knowing that you have the power to rise above these obstacles and welcomeyour true worth and uniqueness. You are deserving of love and acceptance, just as you are. Keep shining your light!

# Overcoming
# Those Obstacles

First, let us cultivate self-awareness through practicing mindfulness practices. Mindfulness meditation can help us become more attuned to our thoughts and reduce the impact of negative self-talk. Engaging in reflective practices like journaling allows us to identify patterns in our thoughts and behaviour, giving us valuable insight.

Next, let us practice self-compassion through self-care activities. By engaging in activities that promote self-compassion, such as exercise, nourishing our bodies with healthy foods, and spending quality time with loved ones, we replenish our emotional well-being. It is important to prioritize self-care regularly and be available for rest and relaxation.

Identifying and extinguishing negative self-talk is another crucial step. Cognitive behavioural therapy techniques can help us identify negative self-talk patterns and reframe them through cognitive restructuring. By practicing positive self-talk and focusing on our strengths and buoyant qualities, we can gradually shift our mindset.

Embracing our imperfection is key to self-acceptance. It is essential to recognize nobody is perfect and that imperfections are a natural part of being human. By practicing self-acceptance and self-forgiveness, we can let go of the need for perfection and instead focus on personal growth and embracing our authentic selves.

Setting healthy boundaries is vital in protecting our well-being. By clearly identifying and communicating our personal boundaries to others, we can create a space that respects and supports our needs. Learning to say "no" to requests that do not align with our values or priorities allows us to prioritize our well-being and cultivate self-love.

By taking these steps, we can overcome the obstacles that stand in the way of self-love and self-acceptance. We will cultivate a deeper sense of self-awareness, self-compassion, and self-acceptance, allowing us to embrace our true worth and live authentically. Remember, this journey takes time and patience, but the rewards are immeasurable. You deserve to love and accept yourself fully, just as you are. Keep moving forward with kindness and compassion towards yourself, and you will find your path to self-love.

## Practicing Self-compassion

Practicing self-compassion is a powerful way of self-love, our emotional well-being, and this allows us to create a loving relationship with ourselves. Personally, I have found the following tips helpful in my own journey.

First, I have become more mindful of my self-talk. It is astonishing how often we can be our own harshest critics. So, when I catch myself engaging in negative self-talk, I consciously try to reframe it with compassion. Instead of berating myself for a mistake, I remind myself that it is human to err and then focus on learning from the experience.

Secondly, treating myself with kindness is transformative. Just as I would care for a dear friend, I carve out time for self-care activities that nurture my mind, body, and soul. Whether it is taking a relaxing bath, pursuing hobbies that bring me joy, or simply giving myself permission to rest and recharge, I prioritize activities that replenish my energy and show myself the love and care I deserve.

Thirdly, self-forgiveness has been an essential practice on my journey. We all stumble and fall along the way, and it is important to remember that these missteps do not define our worth. Embracing self-forgiveness allows me to let go of regrets and move forward with understanding and compassion. It is liberating to acknowledge that our mistakes are opportunities for growth and self-improvement.

Fourthly, eembracing self-acceptance has been a profound shift for me. I have learned to embrace all facets of myself, including my flaws and imperfections. Recognizing that I am worthy of love and respect simply because I exist has empowered me to let go of the constant need for external validation. It is empowering to embrace my authentic self, free from the constraints of societal expectations.

Fifthly, surrounding myself with positivity has also made a significant impact. I choose to spend time with supportive friends and family who uplift and inspire me. I dictate my media consumption, filling my ears and mind with uplifting music, podcasts, and books that fuel my positivity. Engaging in activities that bring me joy, whether it is dancing, painting, or exploring nature, helps me maintain a positive mindset and reinforce self-compassion.

Remember, practicing self-compassion is a journey, and it takes time and effort. Be patient and gentle with yourself as you embrace this new way of relating to yourself. You are deserving of love, care, and acceptance, and by cultivating self-compassion, you can create a foundation of emotional well-being that will support you throughout the ups and downs of your journey through life.

# Identifying and Challenging Negative Self-talk

I have been on a journey to identify and eliminate my negative self-talk, and I am to share what has worked for me. It has not been easy, but I am determined to overcome and to embrace a more positive mindset. The first step becoming more aware of my thoughts throughout the day. I started paying attention to those moments when I found myself thinking, "I'm not good enough" or "I always mess things up." Recognizing these negative thoughts was a powerful first step. I also noticed patterns in my self-talk, like specific situations or triggers that tended to bring it on. Understanding these patterns helped me dig deeper into the underlying causes and address them.

Once I became aware of my negative self-talk, I began challenging those thoughts. I asked myself if there was any evidence to support them. Were they true? I realized that many of these thoughts were based on assumptions or distorted thinking. It was liberating to question their validity and recognize that they did not define my worth or capabilities.

Replacing negative thoughts with positive ones is a crucial practice. Whenever I caught myself in negative self-talk, I would made a conscious effort to replace those thoughts with positive affirmations. I reminded myself of my strengths, accomplishments, and the progress I have made. It took time and practice, but gradually, I started shifting my mindset, creating healthy thought patterns.

Speaking of self-compassion, it has been a game-changer in my journey. I have learned to be kinder to myself, treating myself with the same understanding and forgiveness I would offer to a friend. I remind myself that it is okay to make mistakes and have flaws because we are all human. Showing myself compassion has helped me break free from the cycle of negative self-talk and to instead embrace a more loving and accepting view of myself.

On this journey, I realized that seeking support is not a sign of weakness but a courageous step towards growth. Whenever I need a pick-me-upper, I would reach out to a counsellor, or a trusted friend for guidance, and their fresh perspective has been invaluable in challenging my negative self-talk and providing the support needed to keep moving forward. Probably the most courageous thing I have ever said was, "Help!"

Remember, overcoming negative self-talk takes time and effort. Celebrate every small victory along the way and be patient with yourself. You deserve to experience self-love and embrace positive self-talk. I believe in you, and I am here cheering you on every step of the way. You are stronger than you think, and together, we can conquer those inner doubts and build a more positive and empowering mindset.

# CHAPTER 2

## Setting Healthy Boundaries

Setting healthy boundaries is an essential part of taking care of yourself and maintaining healthy relationships. It is not always easy, but I have learned some methods along the way that have helped me navigate this process.

First and foremost, I have taken the time to reflect on what truly matters to me and what my boundaries are. I have considered my physical and my emotional limits, my values, and my personal preferences. Understanding these aspects of myself has been crucial in defining my boundaries.

Once I have identified my boundaries, I found it important to communicate them clearly and assertively to others. Using "I" statements helps me express my needs without placing blame or making others defensive. For example, saying something like "I need some alone time" or "I am not comfortable with that kind of language" allows me to assert my boundaries while maintaining open communication.

Being firm and consistent while enforcing my boundaries is a game-changer. It is not always easy, especially when others may push against them or assess my resolve. However, by staying firm and consistent, I'm sending a clear message that my boundaries are important and deserve respect.

Sometimes, though, I have found that I need support in my journey, and speaking to someone I trust provided a safe space for me to explore my boundaries, develop strategies for communicating them effectively, and offer guidance on maintaining healthy boundaries in different situations.

Remember, setting healthy boundaries is a form of self-care and self-respect. It takes practice, and there might be challenges along the way, but by prioritizing my well-being and seeking the support I need, I am taking important steps toward building healthier relationships and nurturing my own happiness.

# Improving Self-esteem

# and Self-confidence

Listen closely, as I share this from my heart. Building self-esteem and self-confidence is a transformative journey that can change your life in the most amazing ways. I know because I have experienced this transformation.

Self-compassion is like giving yourself a warm embrace when you need it most. It is being gentle with yourself, accepting your flaws and realizing that you are worthy of love and acceptance. It is not always easy, but when you start treating yourself with kindness, a whole new world of possibilities opens.

Oh, those negative beliefs that have held me back for far too long! I refuse to let them define me anymore. I challenge them with a fiery determination, armed with evidence that proves them wrong. It is time to rewrite the story in my mind and replace those doubts with empowering thoughts. I am capable, I am deserving, and I am ready to conquer those obstacles blocking my path.

Setting goals that push me towards my dreams is like fuel to my inner fire. It is about taking those small steps forward, even when doubts try to hold me back. Each milestone reached is a cause for celebration, a reminder that I am making progress and becoming the person I have always aspired to be.

Taking care of my physical health is an act of self-love that boosts my self-esteem. When I nourish my body with wholesome foods, engage in regular exercise, and honour my need for rest, I feel empowered. I am telling myself that I matter, and I am worth investing in.

Engaging in activities that bring me joy is like unleashing my spirit. When ever I dance, create art, immerse myself in hobbies, a surge of confidence flows through my veins. It is a reminder of my unique talents, passions, and that I am capable of incredible things.

And when the road feels challenging, it is okay to reach out for support. Seeking help is a sign of strength, not weakness. Their wisdom and encouragement provide me with the tools to navigate through my doubts and fears and remind me of the resilient spirit within me.

I said that to better explain this. You are so much more. So much more. And it is time you use that fire that's inside you all along. Shine brightly, that's what we do naturally. Remember that, always. This is our journey to self-discovery. It will have ups and downs, but I open my arm to embrace, and I know you will too. Let us say this together, LOUDLY, "I am strong, I am worthy, and I am ready to unleash my true potential, unapologetically."

## Resilience and the Ability to Cope with Challenges

Bbuilding resilience and coping skills is no walk in the park, but trust me when I say, it is worth every ounce of effort. Life throws us curveballs from left and right, and developing the ability to bounce back and face challenges head-on is liberating. So, let us dive into some tips that have truly made a difference in my own journey.

First things first, I have learned to embrace a growth mindset. Instead of seeing obstacles as roadblocks, I view them as opportunities for evolution. It is like shifting gears in my mind, turning setbacks into steppingstones. It is not always easy, but when I approach challenges with curiosity and a willingness to learn, I come out stronger on the other side.

Speaking of strength, having a solid support network has been a game-changer for me. Surrounding myself with people who honestly believe in me and lift me up during tough times has made all the difference. Whether it is my rock-solid friends, my loving family, or my personal therapist, their support has been the wind beneath my wings when I needed it most.

Self-care has become my secret weapon in building resilience. Taking care of myself physically, mentally, and emotionally has become non-negotiable. From getting regular exercise that gets those endorphins pumping, to nourishing my body with healthy foods, and being available for mindfulness practices, it all adds up. When I prioritize self-care, I am better equipped to manage whatever comes my way.

Mindfulness, my friend, has been a game-changer. It is like having a superpower that keeps me grounded in the present moment. By practicing mindfulness meditation or simply being more aware of my thoughts and emotions, I can better manage stress and anxiety. It is amazing how a few moments of deep breathing can bring a sense of calm amidst the chaos.

When problems arise, I have learned the importance of flexing my problem-solving muscles. Breaking down big challenges into bite-sized pieces and developing a plan of action has helped me feel more in control. It is like being my own superhero, tackling each step and inching closer to a solution. It is empowering, to say the least.

Ahh, negative thinking. It is a tough habit to break, but I have become quite the expert in reframing those negative thoughts. Instead of letting them drag me down, I consciously choose to focus on the positive aspects of a situation or find opportunities for growth and learning. It is like flipping a switch in my mind, shedding light on the silver lining.

And let us remember the power of mistakes. My mistakes used to haunt me, but now I see them as invaluable lessons. When I make a mistake or stumble, I take a step back and reflect on what I can learn from it. It is all about using those experiences to fuel personal growth and create a better path forward. It is a constant journey of improvement, and every misstep is an opportunity to rise higher.

Remember, building resilience and coping skills is a lifelong process. It will not happen overnight, but with persistence and dedication, you will see the incredible transformation it brings. So, take these tips to heart, incorporate them into your daily life, and watch yourself grow stronger and more resilient with each passing day. You have got this!

# Fulfilling Relationships
# with Others

When we create fulfilling relationships, s much more meaning is put into our lives, and that light becomes our life. It is all about those connections that bring happiness, meaning, and a sense of belonging. So, let us dive into some tips that have helped me foster more fulfilling relationships with the people around me.

Listening with purpose is everything. When I practice active listening, I am fully present and focused on the person speaking. I try to understand their perspective and what they are going through. It is about asking open-ended questions and really letting them express themselves without interruptions or judgments. When you make someone feel heard and valued, it can deepen your connection in remarkable ways.

Communication is the backbone of any relationship. I have learned to express my own thoughts and feelings effectively using "I" statements. It is about sharing my needs and emotions without blaming or criticizing others. Instead, I focus on finding solutions and working together as a team. It takes practice, and it creates a safe space for open and honest dialogue.

Empathy is putting myself in someone else's shoes and trying to understand their feelings and needs. It has transformed my relationships. It is about seeing beyond our own perspective and embracing the beautiful diversity of experiences, creating bridges of understanding, and form deeper connections with the people you care about.

Boundaries, setting healthy boundaries is like building a strong fortress for your relationships. I have learned to communicate my boundaries clearly and assertively. And do you know what? It is okay to say no and enforce those boundaries. Being consistent and firm in maintaining them ensures that my relationships are built on mutual respect and understanding.

Gratitude is like a secret ingredient for fostering fulfilling relationships. Expressing appreciation and gratitude for the people in my life has the power to warm hearts and strengthen bonds. Taking a moment to acknowledge their contributions and efforts makes them feel accepted and valued. It is the little acts of gratitude that create big ripples of love.

Shared activities, y bring people closer. Engaging in activities together, whether it is pursuing a shared hobby, playing sports, or being creative, creates memorable experiences. It is in those moments of joy and laughter that deeper connections are forged. So, do not hesitate to create beautiful memories with the people you cherish.

Forgiveness is a gift you give yourself and others. Holding onto resentment and anger can poison relationships. That is why I have learned to practice forgiveness. It is about letting go of past hurts and choosing to move forward with love and understanding. Forgiveness paves the way for healing and allows relationships to even blossom again.

Remember, building more fulfilling relationships is a journey that takes time and effort. It is about embracing open communication, empathy, and a willingness to work through challenges. So, my friend, incorporate these strategies into your daily life and watch your relationships bloom and flourish. Together, let us create a world filled with deep connections and unbreakable bonds.

## Relationships and Connections

The power of nurtureed relationships and connections! There is something truly magical about the way we, as social beings, thrive when we cultivate meaningful bonds with others. It is in those connections where we find solace, support, and a profound sense of belonging.

Nurturing relationships is like tending to a beautiful garden of emotions and experiences. It is about investing our time, energy, and love into the people who hold a special place in our hearts. Whether it is family, friends, colleagues, or even new acquaintances, these connections have the potential to enrich our lives in numerous ways.

When we nurture our relationships, we are we a resending a powerful message to others. We are saying, "You matter to me. I care about your well-being and happiness." By actively listening, we show genuine interest and create a safe space for open and honest communication. It is in these moments of authentic connection that we deepen our understanding of one another and strengthen the bonds that hold us together.

Gratitude and appreciation are the lifeblood of nurturing relationships. Taking the time to express our heartfelt thanks and admiration for the people we cherish can create a profound ripple effect of positivity. When we show appreciation, we uplift their spirits, reinforce the love, and support we have for one another.

Respect and support are the pillars upon which nurturing relationships are built. Respecting each other's boundaries, thoughts, and feelings lays a foundation of trust and mutual understanding. Supporting one another through both triumphs and tribulations strengthens our connection and creates a sense of unity that can weather any storm.

But let us also remember the importance of discernment. Not all relationships are meant to last forever, and that is okay. Some connections may no longer serve our well-being, and it is essential to recognize when it is time has come to make changes. Setting healthy boundaries, engaging in open and honest communication, and making the necessary adjustments for the benefit of both parties are acts of self-care and growth.

The impact of nurtureed relationships and connections is immeasurable. These cherished bonds bring joy, comfort, and a sense of belonging to our lives. They provide a support system that lifts us up during challenging times and celebrates our triumphs. They remind us that we are not alone on this journey, that we are part of something greater than ourselves.

Let us prioritize the nurturing of relationships and connections as an integral part of our personal growth and well-being. Let us listen, appreciate, and support one another. Let us cultivate a garden of love, understanding, and empathy that blooms with every interaction.

Remember, investing in relationships is an investment in our own happiness and fulfillment. It is through these connections that we find the strength to overcome obstacles, the courage to pursue our dreams, and the comfort of knowing we are not alone. So, let us nurture our relationships with passion and intention, and watch as they blossom into something extraordinary.

# Sense of Purpose
# and Fulfillment in Life

Let us focus for a while on finding a sense of purpose and fulfillment in life. Finding purpose and fulfillment in life is like discovering the secret sauce that adds a whole new level of happiness and meaning to everything you do. And guess what? I have some tips that helped me tremendously, and I will share them with you, to help you on your journey.

First things first! Think, dig deep, go way down... explore your core values and beliefs. What makes your heart beats faster? What makes you feel alive and connected to your true self? When you align your actions and goals with these values, it is like unlocking your own personal superpower. You become the hero of your own story!

Next up, when you set meaningful goals is where the magic happens. Picture this: you are on an exciting adventure, chasing dreams that truly light you up. These goals, my friend, they are not just ordinary goals. They are extraordinary. They are the ones that make you stretch, grow, and unleash your full potential. And when you conquer them, the sense of fulfillment is off the charts!

Now let us talk about doing what you love. We are talking about activities that make your soul sing. Whether it is diving into a creative project, dancing like nobody's watching, or exploring the great outdoors, these moments bring pure joy and fulfillment. It is like plugging into an infinite source of energy and passion. You will wonder why you ever settled for anything less!
But guess what? It gets even better. Giving back is where the real magic continues. When you open your heart to others, when you lend a helping hand or make a positive impact in someone's life, that's when purpose hits you like a lightning bolt. Suddenly, you realize the incredible power and you must make a difference. You become a force for good, and that, my friend, is the sweetest kind of freedom.

Now, let us sprinkle some gratitude into the mix. Imagine waking up each day with your heart bursting with gratitude for the blessings in your life. It is like having a superpower that transforms ordinary moments into extraordinary ones. When you shift your focus on all the good things around you, your perspective shifts, and you feel a deep sense of fulfillment.

And always rememberlet us the people who make this journey even more amazing—your tribe. Cultivating meaningful relationships is like having a support system that lifts you higher, cheers you on, and celebrates your wins. These connections are the fuel for your purpose-driven life. Together, you create beautiful memories, inspire each other, and remind one another that you are never alone on this wild ride.

Here comes the grand finale—the job that aligns with your purpose. Picture this: you are doing work that feels like an extension of your soul, where you are making a real impact and loving every minute of it. It is not just about surviving the 9-to-5 grind; it is about thriving and feeling alive in what you do. When you find that perfect match, work becomes an adventure, a playground where you can fully express yourself and leave your mark on the world.

Let us buckle up and embrace this journey. Find your purpose, set those meaningful goals, do what makes your heart dance, give back with all your might, shower gratitude like confetti, and build deep and meaningful connections. And remember, you have got what it takes to create a life filled with purpose, fulfillment, and unshakeable happiness. Get out there and make it happen because you, my love, are destined for greatness!

# CHAPTER 3

## The Power of Our Thoughts

It is truly amazing how our thoughts can shape our entire existence. I have come to realize that our thoughts hold incredible power over our emotions, behaviours, and experiences. Just think about it: negative thoughts can send us spiralling into the depths of anxiety, depression, and a crippling sense of low self-esteem. They can cast a dark cloud over our lives, making every step feel heavy and overwhelming.

But here is the beautiful part, positive thoughts have the power to turn our world upside down—in the best way possible. When we embrace positive thinking, we unlock a wellspring of confidence, self-worth, and motivation within us. Suddenly, we find ourselves standing a little taller, radiating an inner light that attracts success and happiness.

It is not just about our internal landscape, though. Our thoughts shape the lens through which we view the world. If we constantly bombard ourselves with negative thoughts, our perception of the world becomes tainted, as if every corner hides a threat or disappointment. It is no wonder we may feel isolated, trapped in a web of hopelessness. But, when we shift our thoughts to a positive frequency, suddenly the world becomes a magical place brimming with opportunities and untapped potential. We see doors where we once saw walls, and every step forward becomes an adventure filled with endless possibilities.

Here is the fascinating part: our thoughts do not just stay locked within the confines of our minds. They have a profound impact on our actions and behaviours. When we harbor negative thoughts about ourselves, doubts, and insecurities, we unwittingly engage in self-sabotage, holding ourselves back from reaching our true potential. We shrink away from taking risks or stepping out of our comfort zones, settling for a life that is far beneath what we deserve. But when we embrace positive thoughts and beliefs, a whole new world opens before us. We find ourselves filled with a surge of courage and determination, propelling us towards our goals and passions with unwavering conviction.

That is why it is crucial to recognize the incredible power our thoughts wield.

By learning to manage our thoughts and cultivate a positive mindset, we hold the key to unlocking a life that is not only fulfilling but also deeply satisfying. It takes practice, of course, and there will be moments when negativity tries to creep back in. But trust me, my friend, you have the strength within you to reshape your thoughts, to let positivity permeate your every being, and to create a life that brims with joy, love, and infinite possibilities. Embrace the power of your thoughts and watch as your world transforms before your very eyes.

# The Importance Of Positive Thinking

Creating healthy thinking habits is like the secret ingredient that adds a sprinkle of magic to our lives. It is the key to unlocking a world filled with fulfillment, happiness, and endless possibilities. I have come to realize that cultivating a positive mindset is not just a nice-to-have—it is an essential ingredient for living a truly extraordinary life. Let me share with you some reasons why positive thinking is so crucial:

Being intentional about what think about has a profound impact on our mental health. When we embrace positivity, we invite a wave of happiness and contentment into our lives. It is like a shield against the darkness of depression and anxiety. Positive thinking helps lift us up, reducing those heavy burdens and allowing us to see the beauty and joy that surrounds us. It also boosts our self-esteem, reminding us of our inherent worth and greatness.

The wonders of positive thinking don't stop there—it extends its magical touch to our physical health too. It is incredible how our thoughts can influence our bodies. When we embrace positivity, it is as if we are giving our minds permission to heal our physical selves. Our stress levels decrease, inflammation subsides, and our blood pressure finds a calm rhythm. Our hearts beat with newfound strength, and we embark on a journey towards better overall health and well-being.

Let us not forget about the impact positive thinking has on our relationships. When we approach others with warmth, kindness, and empathy, we create a space for deep, meaningful connections to flourish. People are drawn to positive energy like moths to a flame. We become magnets for love, friendship, and support. Our relationships become a source of joy and fulfillment, nurturing our souls, and reminding us of the beauty of human connection.

Life is full of surprises and challenges. But positive thinking gifts us with an extraordinary superpower—resilience. When we encounter obstacles, setbacks, or moments of despair, positive thinking becomes our guiding light. It helps us see beyond the dark clouds, finding silver linings and opportunities for growth and learning. Instead of being weighed down by the burdens we face, we rise above them, like a phoenix reborn from the ashes.

And here is the beautiful truth: positive thinking paves the way for success in all areas of our lives. When we believe in ourselves, our abilities, and our dreams, we become unstoppable forces of nature. We take risks, seize opportunities, and march towards our goals with unwavering determination. With positivity as our driving force, success becomes not just a possibility, but an inevitable outcome.

I urge you to embrace the power of positive thinking. Let it infuse every aspect of your life. Watch as it transforms your mental and physical well-being, kindles deeper connections with others, fuels your resilience, and propels you towards incredible success. With a positive mindset as your compass, your journey through life will be filled with joy, love, and the boundless potential that lies within you. Embrace it, believe in it, and watch as your world unfolds in the most extraordinary way imaginable.

# Managing
# Our Thoughts

To be able to control our thoughts and maintain a positive mindset, now that's a game-changer. I have discovered a few techniques along my own journey that have made a world of difference, and I am excited to share them with you.

First off, let us talk about mindfulness. It is all about being present in the moment, fully aware of your thoughts and feelings without judgment. When those negative thoughts start creeping in, take a deep breath and bring yourself back to the here and now. Notice the beauty around you, the sensations in your body, and let go of those toxic thoughts that try to pull you down...

Another powerful technique is reframing. It is all about shifting your perspective and finding the silver lining in any situation. When a negative thought pops up, challenge it. Ask yourself, "Is this really true? What is a more positive and empowering way to see this?" It is like putting on a pair of rose-tinted glasses and seeing the world in a whole new light...

Now, let us not forget about the power of gratitude. Taking a moment each day to appreciate the good things in your life can work wonders for your mindset. Start a gratitude journal and write down three things for which you are grateful. It could be something as simple as a warm cup of coffee in the morning or a smile from a loved one. By focusing on the positive, you invite more of it into your life...                                  Another that is dear to my heart: self-compassion. We are often our own harshest critics, aren't we? But it is time to be kind to ourselves, to treat ourselves with the love and understanding we would give to a dear friend. When those negative thoughts arise, imagine what you would say to a friend going through the same thing. Then, say those words of love and encouragement to yourself. You deserve it, my friend...

Be around people who are positive. Choose your company wisely and seek out people who uplift and inspire you. Fill your mind with uplifting books, podcasts, and music. Create a positive environment that nurtures your soul and supports your journey towards a positive mindset.

Remember, managing our thoughts and cultivating a positive mindset is a practice. It is not always easy, and there will be moments when those negative thoughts try to sneak in. But with these techniques in your toolbox, you have the power to take control of your thoughts and live a life filled with positivity and joy. You got this, and I am cheering you on every step of the way.

# Creating Positive
# Self-talk Patterns

Let us dive into some practical strategies for creating positive self-talk patterns:

First, it is crucial to be aware of your inner dialogue. Pay attention to the thoughts and statements you make to yourself throughout the day. By becoming aware of negative self-talk, you can start to challenge and change it. Next, challenge the validity of negative thoughts. Ask yourself if there is evidence to support them or if they are based on assumptions. Often, negative self-talk is irrational or distorted. By questioning its accuracy, you can weaken its hold on you.

Replace negative self-talk with positive affirmations. Develop a list of uplifting statements that resonate with you, such as "I am capable," "I am worthy," or "I am resilient." Repeat these affirmations to yourself regularly, especially when negative self-talk arises.
Practice self-compassion. Treat yourself with kindness and understanding, just as you would a dear friend. Offer words of encouragement and support, rather than self-criticism. Embrace your flaws and mistakes as opportunities for growth.

Surround yourself with positivity. Seek out uplifting influences, whether it is reading inspiring books, listening to motivational podcasts, or spending time with supportive friends. Surrounding yourself with positivity can reinforce positive self-talk and help you maintain an optimistic mindset.

Cultivate gratitude and appreciation. Take time each day to reflect on the things you are grateful for and appreciate about yourself and your life. Focusing on gratitude shifts your perspective and encourages positive self-talk.
Celebrate small wins. Acknowledge and celebrate your accomplishments, no matter how small they may seem. Recognizing your efforts and achievements fuels positive self-talk and boosts your confidence.

Creating positive self-talk patterns is a journey that requires consistent effort and practice. Be patient and gentle with yourself as you develop this empowering habit. With time, you will notice a transformation in your mindset and a greater sense of self-belief. Embrace the power of positive self-talk and watch as it shapes a more fulfilling and optimistic life for you.

# Association is Everything

Surrounding ourselves with positive people is crucial for our well-being and self-perception. The company we keep has a profound impact on our mindset, emotions, and overall outlook on life. Here is why it is important to surround ourselves with positivity:

Let us dive deeper. Optimistic people uplift and inspire us. When we are around individuals who radiate positivity, their energy is contagious. They encourage us, offer support, and motivate us to be our best selves. Their optimism and enthusiasm can ignite a spark within us, helping us see the world through a brighter lens.

Positive people also provide a nurturing environment. They create a space where kindness, compassion, and understanding thrive. Being in the presence of such individuals allows us to feel safe, accepted, and valued. This nurturing environment fosters personal growth, self-acceptance, and self-love.

Surrounding ourselves with positivity helps us develop a positive self-image. When we are consistently around people who believe in us, celebrate our successes, and embrace our strengths, we internalize these affirmations. Their belief in us bolsters our own self-confidence and self-esteem. We start to see ourselves in a more positive light and believe in our abilities to overcome challenges and pursue our dreams.

Moreover, positive people influence our mindset and attitudes. They help us cultivate an optimistic outlook on life, even in the face of adversity. When we witness others embracing a positive mindset and finding joy in everyday moments, it inspires us to do the same. Their positive perspectives influence our own thoughts and shape our perception of the world.

Surrounding ourselves with positive individuals also shields us from unnecessary negativity. Negative influences can drain our energy, diminish our self-worth, and hinder our progress. By choosing to surround ourselves with positivity, we create a protective barrier against toxic relationships and harmful influences. We allow ourselves to flourish in an environment that nurtures our well-being and supports our growth.

Remember, it is not about surrounding ourselves with people who are always happy or never experience hardships. It is about surrounding ourselves with individuals who choose to approach life with a positive mindset, who uplift and encourage us, and who genuinely care about our well-being.

By consciously choosing to be in the presence of positive people, we invite positivity into our lives. We amplify our own optimism, strengthen our self-belief, and foster a supportive network that propels us forward. Surrounding ourselves with positivity is not only beneficial to our well-being but also essential for cultivating a healthy self-perception and embracing the beauty of life.

# CHAPTER 4

## Introspection

Let us dive into introspection, where we embark on a journey of self-discovery. Picture yourself sitting down, ready to explore the depths of your own mind, heart, and soul. It is like diving into a pool of emotions, thoughts, and behaviours, eager to unravel the mysteries that lie within.

Introspection is all about turning the spotlight inward and getting to know yourself on a profound level. It is like peeling back the layers of an onion, revealing the core of who you truly are. Through self-reflection and self-analysis, you get a front-row seat to your own inner world. You get to examine your thoughts, emotions, and behaviours, and understand the driving forces behind them.

Why is introspection so important, you ask? Well, it is the gateway to self-awareness, personal growth, and emotional intelligence. By taking the time to explore your inner landscape, you gain a deeper understanding of yourself. You uncover your beliefs, values, and motivations that shape your decisions and actions. It is like finding the missing puzzle pieces that complete the picture of who you are.

Now, let us talk about the techniques you can use to practice introspection. Picture yourself with a journal in hand, pouring your thoughts onto the pages. It is like having a heart-to-heart conversation with yourself, capturing the raw essence of your experiences and reflections. Journaling allows you to see your thoughts come to life, providing clarity and insights that you may have never discovered otherwise.

Guess what, Meditation and mindfulness practices take introspection to a whole new level. Picture yourself sitting in stillness, observing your thoughts and emotions as they arise. It is like becoming the detective of your own mind, unravelling the patterns and stories that shape your perception of the world. Through these practices, you cultivate a deep sense of presence and inner peace, allowing you to navigate life's ups and downs with grace.

Introspection is not about judgment or criticism; it is about self-compassion and growth. It is about embracing all aspects of yourself—the light and the shadow. It is like holding a mirror up to your soul and accepting every part of who you are. Through introspection, you can identify areas for improvement, celebrate your strengths, and embark on a journey of personal evolution.

So, my love, let us embark on this introspective adventure together. Let us dive deep into our thoughts, emotions, and behaviours. Let us uncover the mysteries that make us who we are.

Through journaling, meditation, and mindfulness, we will unveil the treasures hidden within. And remember, introspection is not just a one-time endeavour—it is a lifelong practice that opens doors to self-discovery, growth, and a profound connection with self. Let us embrace this journey and watch ourselves bloom into the incredible beings we are meant to be.

## Practicing Introspection

When it comes to practicing introspection, there are various techniques that can truly be effective, such as:

Journaling: Putting pen to paper and writing down our thoughts, emotions, and experiences can be incredibly insightful. It helps us uncover patterns, identify areas where we may need to make changes, and gain a deeper understanding of ourselves.

Mindfulness meditation: Embracing mindfulness involves being fully present in the moment and observing our thoughts and emotions without judgment. This practice cultivates self-awareness, allowing us to gain clarity and perspective on our inner experience.

Self-reflection questions: Engaging in self-reflection means asking our selves thought-provoking questions that encourage introspection. Questions like "What do I want?" or "What am I grateful for?" prompt us to explore our beliefs, values, goals, and areas for personal growth and improvement.

Self-observation: Sometimes, all it takes is consciously observing our own thoughts, feelings, and behaviours. By paying attention to our body language, noticing our self-talk, or tracking our daily habits and routines, we can uncover valuable insights about ourselves and our patterns.

Seeking feedback: Do not hesitate to seek feedback from others on your thoughts, emotions, and response. Their perspectives can offer fresh insights and highlight blind spots that we may not have noticed on our own. It is a fantastic way to broaden our understanding of ourselves.

# Importance of Shadow-work

Shadow work is something I have personally embarked on, and let me tell you, it has been a journey of self-discovery like no other. It has been about diving deep into the depths of my being and facing the parts of myself that I have kept hidden for so long. It is not always easy, but it is incredibly rewarding.

One of the most powerful aspects of shadow work is its ability to bring healing to our past traumas and negative experiences. By shining a light on those dark corners of our psyche, we can finally acknowledge and release the pain that has been holding us back. It is like lifting a heavy weight off our shoulders and allowing ourselves to move forward with greater freedom and clarity.

Shadow work also helps us develop a profound sense of empathy and compassion. As we explore our own inner struggles and confront our own demons, we start to understand that everyone else is going through their own battles too. It opens our hearts and minds to the human experience in a whole new way, fostering deeper connections and nurturing our relationships.

Engaging in shadow work is not always comfortable. It requires us to face our fears head-on, to challenge our negative beliefs, and to come face-to-face with our flaws. But it is in those moments of discomfort that true growth happens. It is when we embrace our shadows that we become more self-aware, authentic, and empowered individuals.

Shadow work is not a one-time thing, it is an ongoing process, a lifelong commitment to self-discovery and self-acceptance. But let me tell you, the rewards are worth it. As I continue to integrate all aspects of myself, even the parts I once considered undesirable, I find myself living a more fulfilling and meaningful life. I feel more whole, more connected to my true essence.

If you are ready to embark on this transformative journey of shadow work, I encourage you to take that leap. It may be challenging, but it will lead you to a place of profound growth and self-empowerment. Embrace your shadows, embrace your light, and watch as your life transforms in beautiful ways. You have got this!

# Go Deeper

Let us dive into the world of shadow work together and explore some techniques that can support us on this transformative journey. Believe me, I have been there, and I know firsthand the power of these practices. So, if you are ready to commence shadow work, here is how we can get started using various techniques:

Meditation: Find a quiet space, close your eyes, and focus on your breath. Allow yourself to observe any thoughts, emotions, or sensations that arise without judgment. Meditation helps us cultivate mindfulness and creates a safe space to explore our inner landscape.

Journaling: Grab a pen and paper and let your thoughts flow onto the page. Write about your fears, insecurities, and past experiences. Journaling helps us gain clarity, process emotions, and uncover patterns that may be hiding in the shadows.

Yoga and movement: Engage in physical practices like yoga, dance, or any form of movement that resonates with you. Moving your body can help release stuck energy and emotions, providing a pathway for deeper self-exploration. Creative expression: Explore your creativity through art, writing, or music. Expressing yourself creatively can unveil hidden aspects of your shadow and provide a cathartic outlet for emotional release.

Mindfulness: Practice being fully present in the moment. Engage in activities with complete awareness, whether it is savouring a meal, going for a walk-in nature, or simply sitting in silence. Mindfulness helps us observe our thoughts, emotions, and behaviours without attachment.

Therapy or counselling: Consider collaborating with a professional who specializes in shadow work or trauma healing. They can provide guidance, support, and tools to navigate the depths of your psyche.

Self-reflection and introspection: Set aside dedicated time for self-reflection. Ask yourself thought-provoking questions and contemplate your thoughts, beliefs, and behaviours. This deep introspection allows you to explore the hidden corners of your being.

Remember, there is no one-size-fits-all approach to shadow work. Explore these techniques and find what resonates with you. Mix and match them to create a personalized practice that supports your journey of self-discovery and healing.

Embrace the discomfort, trust the process, and allow yourself to transform. Shadow work is a powerful tool for personal growth, and by delving into our shadows, we can embrace our full potential and live more authentically.

Let us take that first step together. Embrace these techniques, be gentle with yourself, and open to the transformative power of shadow work. I believe in you, and I am here to support you every step of the way. You have got this!

# CHAPTER 5

## Forgiveness

You know, forgiveness is something I had to learn the hard way, but it has been a transformative journey. Holding onto anger and resentment was like carrying a heavy weight on my shoulders, weighing me down and draining my energy. It affected not only my emotional well-being but also took a toll on my physical health. I knew something had to change.

When I finally decided to embrace forgiveness, it was a huge turning point. I realized that forgiveness was not about condoning the actions or excusing the hurt caused by others. It was about freeing myself from the pain and reclaiming my power. It was not a painless process, but I knew it was necessary for my own healing and growth.

One of the key realizations on my journey was understanding that we are all human. We all make mistakes and have flaws. The persons who hurt me might have been going through their own struggles, battling their own demons. It did not justify their actions, but it helped me empathize and see them as a complex being, just like me. Forgiving them became an act of compassion, not only for them but for myself as well.

But do you know what? The most challenging part of forgiveness was learning to forgive myself. I did not realize that I had been carrying so much guilt and shame for things that happened in the past. I blamed myself for circumstances that were beyond my control and beat myself up for mistakes I made. It was like a never-ending cycle of self-punishment that prevented me from moving forward.

It took a lot of soul-searching and self-reflection to realize that self-forgiveness was crucial. I had to let go of the notion that I had to be perfect and embrace my own humanity. I had to accept that I am flawed, that I make mistakes, and that is okay. It is a part of being human. Embracing self-forgiveness allowed me to release the guilt and shame and embrace my authentic self, imperfections, and all.

If you find yourself carrying the weight of anger, resentment, or self-blame, consider the transformative power of forgiveness. It is not an easy path, but it is one that leads to liberation and healing. Take your time, be patient with yourself, and know that forgiveness is a gift you give yourself. It is a step towards reclaiming your happiness, peace, and freedom.

Remember, you deserve to live a life free from the burden of past pain. Embrace forgiveness, both towards others and yourself, and watch as it opens new possibilities for love, joy, and growth. You have the strength within you to embark on this journey of forgiveness, and I believe in you wholeheartedly.

# Let Go of Past Hurts

To let go of past pains is necessary when embarking on your healing journey. It is not a straightforward process, but it is incredibly liberating. I want to share with you some techniques that have helped me let go and heal my inner child.

When I forgive and let go, everything for me shifted. Forgiving myself and others does not mean that I am excusing the past or forgetting what happened. It is about releasing the heavy weight of anger, resentment, and hurt that was holding me back. It is like setting myself free from a prison of negative emotions.

I know I'm saying it again, but it is only because it is true. Gratitude has also been a powerful tool in my healing process. Shifting my focus to what I am grateful for helps me appreciate the positive aspects of my life and reduces my attachment to past pain. It is amazing how a simple shift in perspective can bring so much light into my heart.

Mindfulness has played a crucial role as well. By practicing mindfulness techniques like meditation or deep breathing, I have become more aware of my thoughts and emotions. This heightened awareness has allowed me to identify those negative thoughts and emotions connected to past pain, and then consciously choose to let them go. It is a process of releasing what no longer serves me and embracing the present moment.

Engaging in self-care activities has been another vital aspect of letting go of past pain. Taking care of myself physically, emotionally, and mentally has helped me reduce stress and cultivate positive emotions. Whether it is going for a walk-in nature, spending quality time with loved ones, or pampering myself with a soothing bubble bath, self-care has been a powerful antidote to the lingering effects of past pain.

Lastly, seeking counsel has been instrumental in my healing journey. Talking to a therapist provided me with a safe and non-judgmental space to explore my past pain, understand its impact on my present, and develop strategies for letting it go. Having a professional guide, me through the process and support me every step of the way has been invaluable.

Remember love, letting go of past pain is a personal journey. It takes time, patience, and self-compassion. But know that you have the strength within you to heal your inner child and create a brighter future. Embrace forgiveness, gratitude, mindfulness, self-care, and seek support when needed. You deserve to let go of the burdens that are holding you back and embrace a life filled with love, joy, and freedom. You are not alone on this journey, and I believe in you wholeheartedly.

# Let Go of The Guilt

You know, guilt is something I have grappled with personally, and it is a complex emotion that can have a significant impact on our well-being. Let us delve into it together.

Guilt, at its core, is that feeling of responsibility or remorse for something we perceive as an offense, wrongdoing, or mistake. It can serve as a valuable signal, helping us recognize when we have acted in ways that may have harmed others or ourselves. It is a natural part of being human and having a moral compass.

However, there is a fine line between healthy guilt and excessive guilt, especially when it comes to things beyond our control. Excessive guilt over circumstances we could not influence can be detrimental to our mental and emotional well-being. It is like carrying a heavy burden that weighs us down unnecessarily.

When we feel guilty about things beyond our control, it can generate a whirlwind of stress and anxiety. We start questioning ourselves, doubting our worth, and even blaming ourselves for things that were never within our power to change. It is like being trapped in a cycle of negative self-perception, where we forget to acknowledge our limitations and humanity.

Listen, holding onto guilt for things we cannot control robs us of our personal power. It diverts our attention from what we can influence and distracts us from nurturing our well-being. By clinging onto this guilt, we prevent ourselves from focusing on opportunities for personal growth and positive change.

That is why learning to let go of that guilt is crucial for our emotional well-being. When we release ourselves from the weight of guilt associated with things beyond our control, we free ourselves from unnecessary stress and negative emotions. We open the door to self-compassion, allowing ourselves to accept that we are not responsible for everything that happens around us.

Letting go of this guilt empowers us to shift our focus towards the things we can control. It gives us the space to redirect our energy and efforts toward creating positive change in our lives and even the lives of others. It allows us to cultivate a healthier self-image, build resilience, and foster personal growth.

Let go of that guilt, it is not yours to bear. Please understand that you are not responsible for everything that happens in this complex world. Redirect your energy towards what you can control and have influence where it truly matters. By releasing unnecessary guilt, you are creating space for joy, self-acceptance, and personal empowerment. You deserve that freedom! I believe in your ability to let go and embrace a life of emotional well-being.

# Be Kind to Yourself

I have had my fair share of battles with that critical inner voice, and it is something many of us can relate to. Let us dive into this together.

As human beings, we tend to have this internal chatterbox that loves to critique and judge us. To me It is like having a non-stop commentator pointing out our mistakes, flaws, and shortcomings. Sometimes, it feels like this voice is even louder than any external criticism we might receive from others. It isWe appear tobecome our own harshest critics.

Often, we are so quick to blame ourselves for every little mishap and hold ourselves to impossibly high standards. PerhapsIt, is we expect ourselves to be perfect in every way, and when we fall short, that critical voice kicks into high gear. It is exhausting, is it not? This constant self-criticism can chip away at our self-esteem, leaving us feeling inadequate and unworthy.

And let us not forget about the toll it takes on our emotional health. Our self-criticsizing voice loves to pour on us generous helpings of shame and guilt. We start believing that we are inherently flawed or that our mistakes define our worth. This isIt is a heavy burden to carry, my friend, and it can weigh us down, draining our energy and zest for life.

The thing is this self-criticism creates a never-ending cycle of stress and anxiety. We constantly feel the need to prove ourselves, not just to others, but to ourselves as well. Trying to prove ourselves It is like we are on an endless quest for validation and approval, and it can be utterly exhausting.

But here is the beautiful part: recognizing and addressing that inner critic is a game-changer. It is a pivotal step towards being kinder to ourselves and improving our overall well-being. We deserve to treat ourselves with compassion and understanding.

So, let us challenge that critical inner voice together. Let us start by questioning its validity. Are those judgments based on facts or just unrealistic expectations?

Instead of beating ourselves up, let us practice self-compassion. Let us acknowledge that we are human, bound to make mistakes and have flaws. Let us remind ourselves that our worth is not defined by our achievements or how well we measure up to societal standards.

It is time to drown out that critical voice with a chorus of self-acceptance and self-love. Let us celebrate our strengths, even the tiniest ones, and acknowledge our efforts. We do not need to constantly prove ourselves to others or seek validation from external sources.

Love, we deserve kindness and understanding. You are worthy of love and acceptance, just as you are. Embrace your imperfections, for they make you beautifully human. Trust in your journey of growth and self-discovery and know that you have the power to silence that inner critic and nurture a more compassionate relationship with yourself. You are worth it!

# CHAPTER 6

## The Inner Child

I am amazed that connecting with my inner child has been such a profound and transformative journey. I compare it to unlocking a door to my past, where all emotions and memories from my childhood reside. This inner child carries so much weight and influence in my adult life.

You see, my inner child is the vulnerable part of me that experienced pain, neglect, and betrayal during my early years. There is no doubt that those experiences have shaped me more than I realized. They have impacted the way I think, the way I feel, even the way I behave as an adult.

But here is the thing: connecting to my inner child has been the key to personal growth and healing. The effect is like shining a light on those emotional wounds and unresolved issues from my past. By acknowledging and addressing them, I have been able to free myself from their grip and move forward with greater clarity and self-awareness.

When we ignore or neglect our inner child, we are leaving a wounded part of ourselves in the dark. Unfortunately, that darkness can manifest in varying ways. It can show up as anxiety, depression, low self-esteem, and difficulties in our relationships. However, when we open our hearts and embrace our inner child with love and compassion, we create an opportunity for healing and transformation.
Loving and nurturing our inner child is a powerful act of self-compassion. We come to recognize that we deserved love and care back then, and still deserve it now. We realize the importance of It, is validating those emotions and experiences that may have been overlooked or dismissed. We fathom the urgencyIt is of extending a hand to that little version of ourselves and saying, "I see you; I hear you, and I'm here for you."

Connecting to our inner child takes courage and the willingness to expose our vulnerability. I know it is not easy to face those painful memories or it is to confront the dormant emotions that may arise. I also know the rewards are beyond measure, like finding lost treasure by rediscovering our It is sense of wonder, joy, and authenticity that we may have lost along the way.

Hold my hand, are you ready to dive deep within and encourage your inner child to heal those wounds that have been silently shaping your reality? Let us be courageous together and bring light to the darkness and find the path to personal growth and healing. The time has come to befriend our inner child and let our authentic selves shine brightly.

# Healing your Inner Child

Purposefully learning new ways to help my inner child has been a transformative experience. It involves facing head on the wounds and traumas of my past, those experiences that still had a grip, preventing me from living my best life. But the courage to confront and overcome things that we want to forget about, leads to healing and a peace of mind.

You see, those past experiences, those buried emotions, they have a way of lingering in our present. They shape our thoughts, our feelings, and our behaviours, often without us even realizing the damage. They create self-sabotaging patterns, prevent us from reaching our full potential, and strain our relationships with ourselves and with others. But when we heal our inner child, when we address those wounds, the transformation that occurs is awe-inspiring.

Do not be afraid to acknowledge whatever pain you may have. I had to acknowledge my pain. So many of us try to bury those painful memories and emotions, thinking they will just disappear. But in my experience, that is not how it worked. I had to face my past head-on, staring those painful moments in the eye and acknowledging the hurt I experienced. I accepted being vulnerable, to open myself up to those emotions that I had been avoiding for too long. Journaling, meditating, and engaging in mindfulness exercises to reflect on past experiences— were all powerful tools that helped me during the process. And let me emphasize, it is OKAY to seek support during this time.

Now, why is it so important to acknowledge that pain and hurt? Well, my friend, it is because those unresolved issues can hold us back. They can weigh us down and hinder our personal growth. By acknowledging the pain, we gain a deeper understanding of ourselves and the root cause of our struggles. We validate our experiences and give ourselves permission to feel those emotions fully. Without this acknowledgment, we are just running away from our own healing.

So, let us look at techniques that helped me, because healing our inner child requires practical steps.

Journaling became my sanctuary, a place where I could pour out my thoughts and feelings, identifying patterns and triggers related to my past wounds. Mindfulness meditation helped me become more aware of my emotions and physical sensations, teaching me to observe my thoughts without judgment.

For me, therapy was a game-changer. Having a therapist guide me through this process, provided a safe and supportive space. Inner child work, creative expression, support groups—I explored them all, finding what resonated with me and helped me on my healing journey.

But let me be real. In everything, this journey requires patience, and commitment. It requires us to dig deep, to face our fears, and to unravel the stories we tell ourselves. We do not always encounter rainbows and butterflies on the journey, but the rewards are worth it. We can expect inproved emotional well-being, increased self-awareness, and personal growth—these become our companions along the way.

To me, understanding the root cause of those emotional wounds is a game-changer. As we think about our past experiences, beliefs, and behaviours to uncover the source of our pain, clarity emerges. Childhood experiences often play a significant role, whether it is neglect, abuse, or abandonment. These experiences shape our beliefs about ourselves and the world, leading to those negative thought patterns and behaviours.

You will find that understanding the root cause of our pain is like turning on the light in a dark room. It brings clarity and insight to who we are and why we have been carrying our pain for so long. We complete a process of exploration, of being honest and compassionate with ourselves. Sometimes, it requires seeking help from someone who can hold that safe and supportive space for us to heal.

So, let us stick together on this journey of healing our inner child. Together, let us face those wounds, acknowledge the pain, and understand the root causes. It will not always be easy, but I promise you, the transformation and growth that await us are worth every single step. Now is the time to reclaim our power, to heal our hearts, and to embrace the beautiful souls we are meant to be.

# Connecting to your Inner Child

Because I was able to connect with my inner child, self-discovery and healing has been accessible to me. Exploring the experiences and emotions that shaped me as a child and how I subconsciously carried those experiences into adulthood has been life changing.

So, how do we connect with our inner child? Well, the process of visualization has been a powerful tool for me. I close my eyes and imagine myself as that carefree child, playing, laughing, and feeling loved and safe. I picture myself offering comfort and support to that little version of me, showering her with love and understanding.

When I write, the truth always comes out, I was free, so I would say writing played a crucial role for me also. I would grab my journal and pour my heart out on these pages. I wrote a letter to my inner child once, acknowledging her pain, her struggles, and offering the love and support she deserved. Memories and emotions flow onto the paper, creating a bridge between my adult self and the innocent child within.

I also remember doing some inner child meditations. These meditations have been a sanctuary for me. They take me on a journey of visualization and affirmation, helping me feel safe, loved, and connected to my inner child. I Invision wrapping my arms around the little version of me and letting her know that she is seen, heard, and valued.

Of course, it may seem you are riding a rollercoaster of emotions, stirring up memories you thought were buried. You are expected to be constantly demonstrating and accepting compassion and patience, but you will find that it is worth every ounce of your effort.

Learning to eventually understand our emotions is vital, as we begin to reconnect to our inner child. Sadly, many of us were taught to suppress or ignore our feelings, leading to a disconnection from our inner selves. But by acknowledging and accepting our emotions, we can begin to unravel the root cause and work through any underlying issues.

When I consider the role of mindfulness, I realize it has been a game-changer for me. It involves being present in the moment, paying attention to my thoughts and feelings without being judgmental. Through mindfulness, we become more aware of our several emotional states and learn to respond to them in a healthier way.

Set aside time to visualize, write, meditate, and practice mindfulness. Do not hesitate to embrace the emotions, the memories, and the healing that await us. It will not always be easy, but the level of transformation and growth that come from connecting to our inner child are beyond measure. It isBefore it is too late, we must reclaim our innocence, our joy, and our authentic selves.

## Loving your Inner Child

Nurturing my inner child has resulted in such an extraordinary and amazing feeling. A journey of healing and personal growth. It was gratifying to give myself the love and care that I missed during my childhood. Indeed, loving and nurturing myself has been a transformative exit experience.

My guiding light is being able to demonstrate self-compassion. I have learned to treat myself with kindness, just as I would treat a hurting child. I believe that expressing self-care as a way of nurturing my inner child and showing myself the love, I deserve, have been invaluable. It isConsistently giving myself permission to rest, to prioritize my needs, and to be gentle with myself along the way, reinforced loving my inner child.

However, what really hit it home for me, was the power of my inner dialogue. I began talking with my inner child as if she were standing by my side. I softly assured her, "You are loved and safe, and I am here." It may seem a bit silly at first, but it has been incredibly healing. To me, it was an opportunity to re-parent myself and offer the comfort and support that I needed.

Visualization has proven to be another powerful tool in my journey of loving and nurturing my inner child. I close my eyes and imagine that little version of myself, innocent and full of dreams. I give her the biggest hug and whisper words of love and encouragement. I reassure her that she is worthy, that she matters, and that everything will be okay. These moments of visualization bring tears to my eyes, but they are tears of joy, of healing, and of growth.

While this might be weird to you, I have found that it is like pure magic to rediscover the joy of play. I began engaging in activities that used to bring me joy as a child. I purchased art supplies, picked up colouring books, and allowed myself to be silly and imaginative. It is like reconnecting to that inner spark, that sense of wonder and creativity are easily lost in the business of adult life. To me, it was pure bliss.

To connect, forgiveness was one of the first steps I had to take. I learned to forgive myself for any mistake or shortcoming. I have laid down the heavy burden of guilt and shame that I have been carrying for far too long. It is liberating, to set yourself free from the chains of the past and embracing a future filled with self-compassion and growth.

Loving and nurturing my inner child has been the key to unlocking my self-esteem, my self-awareness, and my capacity for healing. The journey entailed unravelling old wounds and replacing them with love and understanding. Trust me when I say it has been worth it, every moment.

I encourage you to embark on your journey of loving and nurturing your inner child. Treat yourself with kindness, have those heartfelt conversations with your inner child, visualize their presence and offer love and comfort. Rediscover the joy of play and let forgiveness wash away any lingering pain. You deserve this healing, this growth, and this self-compassion. Embrace it with open arms and watch yourself flourish.

# Meeting your Future Self

This might sound weird to you, but I was given the opportunity to meet my future self, and it has been a mind-blowing and soul-stirring experience on my journey of personal growth and goal setting. It felt like stepping into a realm of possibilities and envisioning the life I truly desire. I compare visualization to an exercise that fuels my imagination and ignites my motivation to create a future that aligns with my deepest aspirations.

You see, meeting my future self has brought me unparalleled clarity. By immersing myself in this exercise, I gain a clear understanding of what I want to achieve and who I want to become. It is like peering into the depths of my soul and discovering my truest desires and passions. It helps me set goals that resonate with my authentic self and create a roadmap for my journey.

But I will tell you this, something fantastical happens when I meet my self. I begin by going in a comfortable place, I would close my eyes, taking a deep breath, I would transport my mind to a time and place where I have achieved my wildest dreams. I see myself standing there, radiating confidence, wearing a smile that reflects the fulfillment and success achieved. It is a breathtaking moment of visualizing my future self in vivid detail.

I engage all my senses in this visualization. I hear accomplishment and joy surrounding me. I see the vibrant colours of my dream life, painting the canvas of my reality. I touch the textures of achievement and feel the warmth of contentment in my heart. I immerse myself fully in this future moment, embracing the emotions and sensations it brings forth.

I don't only visualize. One of the most beautiful things about this is that I get to have conversations with my future self. I ask questions about how I achieved my goals, what obstacles I overcame, and what wisdom I gained along the way. The experience is like tapping into a well of infinite knowledge and receiving guidance from my own wise and accomplished mentor. My future self shares insights, lessons, and advice that inspire me to take steps forward more confidently.

I take it all in, absorbing every word and allowing it to permeate my being. The motivation that surges within me is unparalleled. I feel a profound sense of accountability as I witness the potential consequences of my current actions. I am driven to make choices and decisions that align with the future I have envisioned, propelling me closer to my dreams.

Meeting my future self also grants me a new perspective on my present circumstances and challenges. It helps me navigate through the complexities of life with a long-term vision in mind. I do not get caught up in short-term gains or temporary setbacks. I keep my eyes fixed on the horizon, unwavering in my commitment to realizing my goals.

This exercise builds resilience like nothing else. It instillswithin me an unwavering determination to push forward, even in the face of adversity. I hold onto the image of my future self, knowing that no matter what hurdles may come my way, I have the strength and tenacity to overcome them.

If you would like to join me on this transformative journey of meeting your future self, find a quiet and comfortable space to dive deep into your imagination. Close your eyes, take those deep breaths, and transport yourself to a future moment of triumph and fulfillment. Engage all your senses, ask those provocative questions, and be inspired by the wisdom that flows from your future self.

when you return to the present, remember to capture the insights and inspiration that arose during this exercise. Write them down, reflect on them, and let them guide you on your path towards personal growth and goal achievement. You have the power within you to create a future beyond your wildest dreams. Embrace the opportunities of meeting your future self and unleash your potential.

# Ask your Future Self

Here are some questions I have personally found valuable to ask my future self when we meet:

• What accomplishments are you most proud of?

• What goals did you set for yourself and achieve?

• How did you overcome obstacles or setbacks?

• What did you learn from your failures and mistakes?

• What values and principles do you live by?

• What advice would you give to your younger self?

• How have you grown and changed as a person?

• What new experiences have you had?

• What relationships have been most important to you?

• What brings you the most happiness and fulfillment in your life?

# Set Goals and Take Action

Upon identifying my passions and values, the next exciting step in walking in my purpose is to set goals and wholeheartedly take-action towards achieving them. Setting clear and specific goals allows me to channel my energy and efforts towards manifesting what I truly desire in life.

To make the goal-setting process more manageable and motivating, I have learned to break down my goals into smaller, achievable tasks. This way, I can track my progress, celebrate each milestone, and keep my motivation soaring high.

Creating a timeline is another vital aspect of goal setting. By setting specific time frames for each goal, I avoid procrastination, and maintain focus and a sense of urgency that propel me forward.

When it comes to prioritizing my goals, I ensure to discern which hold the most significance for me. In this way, I can concentrate my efforts on those goals that truly align with my purpose and values, making sure I invest my time and energy where it matters most.

Holding myself accountable is powerful in my goal-setting journey. I take full responsibility for my progress by tracking my achievements, acknowledging, and celebrating my successes along the way, and making necessary adjustments to stay aligned with my vision.
But dreams and setting goals alone will not bring about the transformation I seek. Acting is the pivotal step that turns my dreams into reality. I understand that progress is achieved through consistent and deliberate effort, even if it means taking small steps each day. Each action I take, no matter how seemingly insignificant, contributes to the grand tapestry of my success.

Setting goals and acting on them, fuelled my journey towards a purposeful life. I am empowered to navigate the path of personal growth and fulfillment. By remaining steadfast in my pursuit, I am confident that I will embrace the life I envisioned and become the best version of myself. So, I strongly encourage setting goals, igniting passion, and fearlessly acting on the beautiful journey of purposeful living.

# Understand your Emotions

Let us infuse some motivational energy into understanding our emotions and connecting with our inner child. You hold within you an incredible power – the power to understand and embrace your emotions. Remove the strain on your power and connect with your inner child on a profound level!

In the past, you might have been taught to suppress or ignore your feelings, but today, you are breaking free from that suppression. Now, you are ready to dive headfirst into the realm of emotions and reclaim your emotional authenticity.

Mindfulness: The Keys to Unlocking Emotional Awareness
Imagine the possibilities that await when you practice mindfulness! By becoming fully present in each moment, you open the door to a deeper understanding of your emotional make up. Mindfulness empowers you to observe your thoughts and feelings without judgment, allowing you to tap into your emotional intelligence like never before.

As you cultivate this awareness, you will discover a treasure trove of insights into the root causes of your emotional expressions. You will gain clarity on why certain feelings arise, and this newfound understanding will become a catalyst for personal growth and healing.

Journaling: Your Pathway to Self-Discovery

Grab that pen and journal – it is time to unleash your inner storyteller! Through the art of journaling, you embark on a transformative journey of self-discovery. With every stroke of the pen, you bring your thoughts and emotions to life on the page, revealing the depths of your inner self.

Through journaling, you will uncover patterns and recurring themes in your emotions, illuminating the path towards self-awareness. This practice becomes a powerful tool for reflection and self-expression, enabling you to connect intimately with your inner child. As you pour your emotions onto the page, you are reclaiming your voice and acknowledging any unresolved feelings that have long yearned to be released.

A Journey of Growth and Healing...

While this journey may not always be easy, remember, the most profound transformations occur as we venture outside our comfort zones. By understanding your emotions, you are nurturing your inner child and facilitating personal growth on a whole new level.

You are peeling back the layers, embracing the full spectrum of your emotions, and embarking on a path of healing. With each step forward, you are reclaiming your emotional authenticity and paving the way for a brighter, more fulfilling future.

So, my friend, let your emotions guide you, for they hold the keys to unlocking your true potential. Dive into mindfulness and journaling with unwavering determination. Embrace the challenges that come your way, knowing that they are steppingstones on your journey towards emotional well-being and self-discovery.

Remember, you are capable, resilient, and ready to embark on this empowering journey. Connect with your inner child, understand your emotions, and watch as you rise to new heights of personal growth and fulfillment. The power is within you, to expressed, and release. Now, go out there and make your emotional dreams a reality!

# CHAPTER 7

## Over Come Fear and Self-doubt

I know first-hand how challenging it can be to overcome fear and self-doubt. Lol, I'm still going through it all now! The weight they can hold us back from embracing our true selves, from chasing our dreams with unyielding passion. But let me tell you this: You have the power within you to conquer these formidable adversaries. Together, we will rise above them.

First, let us go deep into the core of your fears and self-doubts to understand their origin and unravel their tangled roots. By shining a light on these hidden corners of your psyche, you gain the upper hand. You begin taking control of your narrative, refusing to let fear and doubt define your path.

Next, we challenge those negative thoughts that threaten to undermine our confidence. Stand firm and question their validity. Are they based on concrete facts or merely assumptions? Replace those destructive thoughts with powerful affirmations that resonate with your soul. Remind yourself of your worth, your capabilities, and the incredible potential that resides within you.

As you embark on this journey, remember to be gentle with yourself. Practice self-compassion, recognizing your flaws and imperfections as integral parts of your unique self. Treat yourself just as you would a cherished friend, with unwavering kindness and understanding. You are worthy of love and acceptance, both from others and from within your being.

Now, it is time to be courageous and take those steps beyond the boundaries of your comfort zone. Begin with small, deliberate actions that push the limits of what feels safe. With each victorious stride, celebrate your triumphs, no matter how seemingly insignificant. Recognize that growth resides just outside the realm of familiarity, and that's precisely where you need to be.

Shift your focus to your strengths. Acknowledge your past achievements, no matter how humble they may seem. Cherish the unique gifts that make you who you are. They are the armor that shields you from doubt and ignites the fire of confidence within your soul. Cling to them fiercely and let them guide you forward.

In times of doubt, reach out for support. Share your fears and uncertainties with trusted friends, family, or perhaps seek solace in the knowledge or wisdom of a therapist. Their empathy and guidance will provide insightful perspectives that may have eluded you. Remember, you are not alone on this journey. Together, we can overcome the shadows that attempt to overshadow your light.

Overcoming fear and self-doubt is a process, an ever-evolving dance with your inner self. You must exhibit patience, perseverance, and unwavering belief in your own potential. Trust the process and honor the progress you make, no matter how small it appears. Keep moving forward courageously, one step at a time.

You can achieve greatness, my friend. Connect to your true power and let it propel you towards the life you've always envisioned. Fear and self-doubt may linger, but they will no longer hold dominion over your spirit. Stand tall, face your fears head-on, and watch as you emerge victorious on the other side.

Believe in yourself, for I believe in you. Together, we will conquer fear, silence self-doubt, and pave the way for a future where your brilliance shines unapologetically. You have the strength within you. You can soar.

# Walk in Your Purpose

Walking in my purpose is like dancing to the rhythm of my soul. It is a vibrant and electrifying way of living that fills every Fiber of my being with passion, emotion, and a sense of profound connection. It means chasing after the things that set my heart on fire, the things that make me come alive. It is about connecting to my deepest passions, unwavering values, and unique strengths to create a life that feels like a masterpiece—a life that leaves an indelible mark on the world.

Discovering my purpose is not just about finding some elusive destination; it is about embarking on a thrilling journey of self-discovery and self-expression. It is about unearthing the treasures buried within me, the passions that ignite like a wildfire in my soul. I become excited when exploring the realms of my heart and my mind, and participating in   activities and experiences that make time stand still. Whether it is writing, painting, singing, or lending a helping hand to those in need, I follow the path that lights up my spirit.

But it is not just about passions; it is about honouring my core values as well. These are the guiding principles that anchor me, the compass that points me in the right direction. Integrity, compassion, authenticity—these are the virtues that resonate within me, urging me to make a positive impact on the world. They remind me that my purpose is not just about personal gratification; rather encompasses using my unique gifts and talents to contribute to something greater than myself.

Walking in my purpose fills me with an unstoppable drive and determination. To me It is like a surge of electricity coursing through my veins, propelling me forward even in the face of challenges and self-doubt. Yes, there are moments of uncertainty and fear, but I refuse to let them hold me back. I welcome the unknown, for I know that growth and transformation reside just beyond my comfort zone. I take bold leaps and courageous steps, trusting that my purpose will guide me and provide the necessary strength and resilience.

Every action I take is infused with intention; every decision guided by my vision. I am in tune with my innermost desires and aspirations, and I allow them to light my path. I celebrate my strengths and accomplishments, recognizing that they are the building blocks of my purposeful existence. And even when setbacks arise, I view them as valuable lessons and steppingstones towards reaching my fullest potential.

Walking in my purpose brings an unparalleled sense of fulfillment and contentment. It is like a symphony of joy playing in my heart, reminding me that I am living a life aligned with my truest self. I am energized by the knowledge that my actions have a ripple effect, touching the lives of others and making a difference in the world. To me, it is not about seeking external validation; I believe it is about finding solace and satisfaction in knowing that I am making my mark, no matter how small or grand.

So, I invite you to join me on this exhilarating journey of purpose. Let us dive deep into our passions, unleash our creativity, and make a positive impact on the world. Let us dance to the beat of our own drums, fearlessly expressing who we are and unleashing the potential within us. The world is waiting for our unique contributions, and together, we can create a symphony of purpose that reverberates throughout time. Embrace your purpose!

## Stay True to Who You Are

Let me share something, staying true to who I am is not just a choice I made—it is a way of life. Each moment is like breathing in the purest, most authentic air and exhaling everything that doesn't serve me. Being true to myself means I refuse to conform to the expectations and opinions of others. I am the captain of my own ship, navigating through life guided by my own compass.

When I stay true to myself, I am not afraid to let my true colours shine. I embrace my quirks, my passions, and my beliefs with unwavering conviction. I am not here to please everyone or fit into society's neat little box. On the contrary, I am here to embrace my individuality, to celebrate my uniqueness, and to walk my own path.

There are moments when the world tries to pull me in different directions, urging me to conform and blend in. But let me tell you something: I will not back down. I will not compromise my values or passions just to please others. I stand tall, unapologetically me, even when it feels like I am swimming against the current.

Being true to myself is more than just a superficial act—it is rooted in a deep sense of self-awareness. I know who I am at my core, what I believe in, and what sets my soul on fire. I have taken the time to peel back the layers, to go deeper into the depths of my being and uncover my true essence. It is a journey of self-discovery, and it is worth every moment.

And do you know what is beautiful? When I stay true to myself, I attract the right people into my life—those who appreciate me for who I am, without judgment or expectation. Genuine connections are forged because I am not putting on a show or pretending to be someone I am not. I am building relationships based on trust, acceptance, and mutual respect. These are the kind of connections that light up my world and make me feel truly alive.

Sure, there are times when doubt and insecurity creep in. The world can be loud and relentless, bombarding me with its beliefs and standards. But in those moments, I take a deep breath and remind myself of my worth. I remind myself of the strength and courage it takes to stay true to who I am. I surround myself with positive influences and uplifting voices that remind me of my power and potential. So, my friend, I invite you to join me on this journey of authenticity. Embrace every part of who you are—the strengths, the weaknesses, the passions, and the dreams. Do not let anyone else define your worth or dictate your path. Trust yourself, trust your intuition, and let your true self shine brilliantly.

Remember, staying true to who you are is not always easy, but it is worth it. Consider it as a testament to your courage, resilience, and unwavering spirit. Embrace your uniqueness, honour your values, and let your authenticity be a guiding light in a world that needs more genuine souls.

Stay true to yourself and watch as you create a life that is a true reflection of your magnificent, authentic self. You deserve nothing less.

# Embrace your Uniqueness

Let me tell you something, my friend. Embracing your uniqueness is like stepping into a power that is entirely your own. You must honour the beautiful tapestry of traits, quirks, and talents that make you who you are. Learn to celebrate the fact that there is no one else on this planet quite like you.

We live in a world that constantly tries to fit us into predefined boxes, pressuring us to be like everyone else. But let me ask you this: why would you want to be a copy when you were born an original? Embracing your uniqueness is a rebellion against the mundane and a declaration of your authentic self.

When you embrace your uniqueness, you unlock a world of possibilities. You give yourself permission to shine in your own extraordinary way. You stop comparing yourself to others and start appreciating the one-of-a-kind qualities that set you apart. You will realize it is in those unique qualities that your true power lies.

Welcome your uniqueness is not about seeking validation or approval from others. On the contrary, it is about finding acceptance and love within yourself. By then, you begin to realize that you don't need to conform to societal standards to be worthy or successful. Your worthiness is innate, and your success is defined by your own terms.

The benefits of embracing your uniqueness are immeasurable. When you fully accept and love yourself for who you are, you radiate confidence and authenticity. People are naturally drawn to those who embrace their uniqueness because they consider it refreshing and inspiring. You become a beacon of light, encouraging others to embrace their own uniqueness and break free from the chains of conformity.

Embracing your uniqueness also opens doors to new opportunities. When you step into your authentic self, you attract experiences and connections that align with your true essence. You find yourself in environments where your strengths are valued and celebrated. Life becomes a vibrant tapestry of exploration and growth, as you navigate through paths that were meant for you and YOU, alone.

But let us be real for a moment. Embracing your uniqueness can be scary. It means stepping outside of your comfort zone and facing the fear of judgment or rejection. But here is the truth: the greatest opportunities to grow happens outside of your comfort zone. In those moments of vulnerability that you discover the depths of your resilience and the unlimited expanse of your spirit.

So, I urge you to grasp your uniqueness with all your heart. Celebrate your quirks, your passions, your talents— everything that makes you beautifully different. Do not be afraid to stand out, to shine brightly, and to be unapologetically you. The world needs your unique voice, your unique perspective, and your unique gifts.


Remember, you were born to be different. Accept it. Cherish the freedom that comes with being true to yourself. Welcome the joy of living a life that is a genuine reflection of who you are. Embrace your uniqueness, my friend, and watch as your world transforms into a kaleidoscope of endless possibilities.

# Navigate External Influences

Let us talk for a moment about navigating external influences, because let me tell you, it is a game-changer. In this world of constant noise and opinions, it is so easy to get lost in the sea of other people's expectations and judgments. But here is the thing: your life is yours to live, and it is time to take the wheel.

Navigating external influence is all about taking control of your own destiny. It is about making conscious choices based on your own values, desires, and dreams, rather than blindly following the crowd. It means being mindful of the influence that others have on you and being intentional about the impact it has on your life.

When you navigate external influences, you reclaim your power and become the author of your own story. You no longer let the opinions of others define who you are or what you should be. Instead, you tune in to your inner voice, that beautiful compass that knows what truly resonates with your soul.

By embracing the importance of navigating external influences, you create a life that is authentic to your true self. You break free from the shackles of societal norms and expectations, and you start living on your own terms. It is a liberating feeling, my friend, to finally be able to say, "This is who I am, and I'm damn proud of it."

Of course, navigating external influence is not always easy. We require courage, self-awareness, and a whole lot of resilience. You will face moments when the pressure to conform feels overwhelming, when the fear of judgment paralyses you. But trust me, those moments are precisely when you need to dig deep and hold on to your authenticity with all your might.

The benefits of navigating external influence are tremendous. When you live life on your own terms, you experience a sense of tremendous freedom like no other. You make choices that align with your values and aspirations, leading to a life filled with purpose and fulfillment. Your actions become a reflection of your true self, and you radiate an aura of authenticity that inspires others to do the same.

Navigating external influences also allows you to cultivate deep and meaningful connections. When you embrace your authentic self, you attract people who appreciate you for who you truly are. You create a tribe of individuals who love and support you unconditionally, because they recognize the beauty of your uniqueness. These connections nourish your soul and bring joy and fulfillment into your life.

We will navigate this journey of life with our heads held high and always being mindful of the external influences around us, while filtering out the noise that does not align with our truth. We will listen to our inner voice, that wise guide that knows what is best for us. We will make choices that honour our values, dreams, and passions.

Remember, this is your life, and you have the power to create a masterpiece. Embrace the importance of navigating external influences, and watch your life transforms into a vibrant tapestry of authenticity, purpose, and genuine happiness. The world is waiting for you to shine your unique light. Come along, my friend. Let us navigate this journey together.

## The Scarcity Mentality- LET IT GO!

Okay, let us have a heart-to-heart about something that something that constantly plagues us; letting go of the scarcity mentality. You know what I am talking about – that mindset that constantly whispers in your ear, "There is not enough. You will never have what you want. You better hold on tight to what you've got."

But I will tell you this, living with a scarcity mentality is like living in a tiny, cramped box. It keeps you trapped, afraid, and always wanting more. The time has come to break free from that suffocating mindset and choose a world of abundance and limitless possibilities.

When you let go of the scarcity mentality, you open yourself up to a whole new way of living. Instead of focusing on what you lack, you start seeing the abundance that surrounds you. You realize that there is enough love, success, and opportunities to go around – and that includes you.

By shifting your mindset to one of abundance, you tap into the infinite potential that resides within you. You recognize that your worth is not determined by external circumstances or material possessions. Your worth comes from within, and it is boundless.

Letting go of the scarcity mentality allows you to embrace a mindset of gratitude. You start appreciating the blessings and abundance that already exist in your life. You become aware of the small miracles and joys that surround you every single day. Gratitude becomes your superpower, amplifying the positive energy and attracting even more abundance into your life.

But here is the kicker! Letting go of the scarcity mentality does not mean sitting back and waiting for things to magically appear. Rather, it is about taking inspired action, stepping out of your comfort zone, and trusting in the abundance of the universe.

When you release the grip of scarcity, you give yourself permission to dream big and go after what you truly desire. You stop settling for mediocrity and start believing that you deserve greatness. You take risks, pursue your passions, and open yourself up to a world of endless possibilities.

My friend, the benefits of letting go of the scarcity mentality are truly life changing. You experience a newfound sense of freedom, joy, and fulfillment. Your relationships deepen as you let go of competition and comparison, and instead, embrace collaboration and support. You attract opportunities and experiences that align with your authentic self, propelling you towards your wildest dreams.

The time has come to break free from the chains of scarcity. Choose abundance. Choose to believe in yourself and the infinite possibilities that await you. Trust that there is more than enough to go around, and that you are worthy of all the blessings that come your way.

You are not defined by scarcity. You are defined by your limitless potential and the love that flows through your heart. Embrace the abundance that surrounds you and watch as your life transforms into a tapestry of blessings, fulfillment, and extraordinary growth.

Now is the time to step into a world of abundance. Are you ready?

## Belief and Mindset

Let us consider the awe-inspiring power of belief and mindset! It is incredible how what we believe, deep down in our core, can shape our entire reality. Our beliefs are like the lenses through which we perceive the world, and they have the remarkable ability to either lift us up to incredible heights or hold us back in the shadows.

Belief is the spark that ignites the fire within us. Our unwavering conviction that propels us forward, even in the face of adversity. When we honestly believe in ourselves, in our dreams, and in our abilities, the universe conjoins in our favour. In applause the doors of opportunity swing wide open, inviting us to step into a world of infinite possibilities.

However, I am not just talking about blind belief. The belief I am referring to involves cultivating a mindset that aligns with our deepest desires and aspirations. Our mindset is the fertile soil in which our beliefs take root and flourish. The lens through which we interpret the world and the lens through which the world responds to us.

A positive mindset is our superpower. We project the unwavering belief that obstacles are merely steppingstones, challenges are opportunities for growth, and setbacks are temporary detours on the path to success. With a positive mindset, we can conquer mountains, overcome hurdles, and transform setbacks into comebacks.

But here is the secret sauce: our beliefs and mindset are not fixed or predetermined. They are like muscles that we can train and strengthen. We have the power to reframe our beliefs, challenge our self-imposed limitations, and adopt empowering thoughts and beliefs that serve our greater good.

It starts with our awareness. We must become conscious of the thoughts that swirl in our minds and the beliefs that shape our reality. Are they lifting us up or dragging us down? Are they propelling us forward or holding us back? By shining a light on our beliefs, we can identify the ones that no longer serve us and replace them with beliefs that empower us to reach new heights.

Belief and mindset are not just about positive thinking; they are about deep-rooted faith in ourselves and in the universe. They are about trusting that everything happens for a reason, even when we cannot see the bigger picture. We accept the notion that we are the architects of our own destiny, and that our thoughts and beliefs create the blueprint for the life we want to live.

So, let us cultivate a belief system and mindset that elevate us. Let us banish self-doubt, fear, and self-limiting beliefs from our minds. Instead, let us embrace unwavering faith, resilience, and the unshakable belief that we can achieve greatness.

Remember, what we believe shapes our reality. Our beliefs and mindset can either be our greatest allies or our harshest adversaries. So, let us choose beliefs that empower us, thoughts that uplift us, and a mindset that propels us towards our dreams. With the right belief and mindset, we have the power to conquer any obstacle, overcome any challenge, and create a life that surpasses our wildest dreams. Believe it, my friend, and watch as the world transforms around you.

# CHAPTER 8

## Set Clear Intentions

Let us delve into a topic that can truly transform your life: setting clear intentions. Let us picture this. You are sailing in a vast ocean without a destination in mind. You are just drifting, going wherever the currents take you. But what if I told you that you have the power to steer your ship, to chart your own course, and to arrive at a destination that aligns with your deepest desires?

Setting clear intentions is like following a compass that guides you towards the life you genuinely want to live. You are the one defining your purpose, clarifying your goals, and infusing every action with meaning and direction. When you set clear intentions, you declare to the universe and to yourself what you want to experience, achieve, and become.

Intention is like the fuel that propels your dreams into reality. With it, you transform mere wishes into tangible results. Without clear intentions, you are just drifting through life, reacting to whatever comes your way or where you end up. But when you set intentions, you take charge. You become the captain of your own ship, steering towards your desired destination.

Setting clear intentions empowers you to make conscious choices. You better focus your energy, attention, and resources on what truly matters to you. When you have a sharp vision of your intentions, it becomes easier to say "yes" to opportunities that align with your goals and values, and to say "no" to distractions that veer you off course.

And here is the beauty of it all: setting intentions is not just about achieving external success or acquiring material possessions. You are aligning your life with your deepest values and desires. It is about living in harmony with your authentic self, and experiencing joy, fulfillment, and inner peace.

When you set clear intentions, you become a magnet for positive energy and synchronicities. The universe concurs to support you on your journey, bringing forth the right people, circumstances, and opportunities to propel you forward. Doors open, paths unfold, and serendipitous moments become a regular occurrence. It is as if the whole universe is cheering you on, saying, "You've got this!"

But let us also remember the emotional aspect of setting clear intentions. You are connecting with your heart's desires and infusing your intentions with passion, emotion, and purpose. When you set intentions from a place of authenticity and in alignment with your desires, they become infused with your unique essence. They become a reflection of who you truly are and what you want.

Please, take a moment to reflect on what you truly desire in life. What ignites your soul? What makes your heart sing? Set clear intentions that resonate deep within you. Write them down, speak to them aloud, or hold them in your heart. Cling on to them with unwavering belief and unwavering trust.

And remember, setting clear intentions is not a one-time event. It is an ongoing practice. As you evolve and grow, your intentions may shift and expand. Stay open, stay flexible, and remain attuned to your acquired wisdom.

You have the power to shape your life, my friend. You can set clear intentions that create a ripple effect of transformation. Embrace this power, trust in the process, and watch as the transition unfolds before your eyes.

Are you ready to set sail towards your dreams? The journey awaits. Set your intentions, my friend, and let the adventure begin!

## Manifest the Life You Want

It should be gratifying when you are manifesting the life you want. Buckle up, as we areto take a trip that will blow your mind and ignite your soul!

First things first, let us talk some more about mindset, and reiterating the power of belief. Your mindset is like the captain of your ship, steering the course of your life. It is the lens through which you perceive the world and then your beliefs help to shape your reality. And here is also some exciting news: with the right mindset, manifesting the life you want is achievable!

What is so magical about the mindset about which I am talking? Well, it is the belief that you are the creator of your own reality. It is the unwavering conviction that you have the power to shape your life according to your desires and dreams. This coupled with the understanding that your thoughts, emotions, and actions have the ability to attract and bring into manifestation your deepest desires.

When you genuinely believe in the power of manifestation, you unleash an unstoppable force within you. You tap into the infinite potential that resides within your being. You become a co-creator with the universe, working hand in hand to bring your dreams to life.

But here is the catch: manifesting the life you want requires more than just wishful thinking. It demands an unwavering commitment and an unshakable belief in your own power. It calls for clarity, focus, and action.

To manifest the life you want, you must start by getting clear on what it is you desire. Visualize it, feel it, and believe it with every Fiber of your being. The more specific and detailed you are, the stronger the signal you send out to the universe.

Next comes the fun part: aligning your thoughts, emotions, and actions with your desires. Cultivate positive thoughts and beliefs that support your vision. Let go of self-doubt and limiting beliefs that hold you back. Surround yourself with people and resources that uplift and inspire you.

But it does not stop there. You must embody the energy of what you desire. Feel the joy, the excitement, and the gratitude as if your dreams have already come true.

Function as if you are living the life, you desire and watch as the universe responds in kind.

And here is a little secret: the universe loves speed. Take inspired action towards your goals. Break down your dreams into manageable steps and start taking consistent action. Trust that the universe will meet you halfway, providing opportunities and synchronicities along the way. Now, I will not sugar-coat it. The path to manifesting your dreams may have its twists and turns. You may encounter challenges and setbacks. But remember, every obstacle is an opportunity for growth and learning. Embrace the journey, stay persistent, and keep your eyes on the prize.

And here is one of the most incredible parts: when you believe in the possibility of manifesting the life you want, you notice miracles unfolding around you. Synchronicities become a regular occurrence. Doors open where you least expect them. The right people and resources come into your life at the perfect time.

So, I invite you to embrace the power of manifestation. This my friend is an open invitation. Believe in your dreams. Trust in your own creative abilities. Set your intentions, align your thoughts and actions, and watch as the universe cooperates to make your dreams a reality.

Remember, you are the author of your own story. The pen is in your hands, and the possibilities are limitless. With the right mindset, the world is your playground, and your dreams are within reach.

Get ready to manifest the life you want, my friend. It is time to unleash your magic and create the reality you have always envisioned. The universe is waiting to support you on this incredible journey. So, let us go!

# Trust God

Let us go a bit deeper and talk about the incredible power of faith and trusting in God's divine timing. Get ready to feel the fire in your soul as we explore how having God at the forefront of our lives leads to a balanced and fulfilling existence.

You see, faith is the anchor that keeps us grounded when life throws its curveballs. Let it be the unwavering belief that there is a higher power guiding our paths and orchestrating every step of our journey. When we place our trust in God, we surrender our worries and fears, knowing that He has a perfect plan for us.

Having faith does not mean life will be smooth sailing all the time. Oh no, it is quite the opposite. We will face challenges, setbacks, and moments of uncertainty. But here is the beautiful truth: when we have faith, we tap into an unshakable inner strength that helps us navigate through the storms of life.

When we surrender to God and to his timing, we let go of our need to control every aspect of our lives. We embrace the truth that His timing is perfect, even if it does not align with our own plans. We learn to wait patiently, knowing that God's plans far exceed our limited understanding.

You see, faith and trust in God bring balance to every aspect of our lives. When we prioritize our spiritual well-being, everything else falls into place. Our relationships become deeper and more meaningful as we love and forgive as God does. Our work becomes purposeful and fulfilling as we seek to serve and make a positive impact. Our minds find peace and clarity as we surrender our worries to him who holds the universe in His hands.

Having a balanced life means aligning our priorities with God's will. It means seeking His guidance in every decision we make, big or small. It means dedicating time to prayer, to reflect, and to worship, all the while, nourishing our souls and drawing closer to our Creator. It means treating ourselves and others with love, compassion, and kindness, mirroring the grace and mercy God has shown us.

You may find this surprising but let me be real with you. Living a life of faith and trust in God does not exempt us from challenges or hardships. We will face trials that evaluate our faith and experience moments where we question God's plan. But in those moments, we must remember that our faith is not weakened by doubts but strengthened by them. It is in those times of uncertainty that our faith deepens and our trust in God's wisdom grows.

So, my dear friend, I encourage you to embrace the power of faith and trusting in God. Let Him be the centre of your life, guiding your steps and filling your heart with peace and purpose. Surrender your worries, your fears, and your need for control, and watch as God orchestrates miracles in ways you never imagined.

With faith as your compass, you will navigate the highs and lows of life with grace and resilience. Your relationships, your work, your mind, and your soul will find harmony and balance. Trust in God's perfect timing and watch as He unfolds His blessings in your life.

Remember, trusting in God is not a guarantee that life will be easy, but it is an assurance that you will never walk alone. So, take a leap of faith, let go of being in control, and enjoy the beautiful journey of a balanced life in His loving bosom.

# Gratitude and Appreciation

There is another source of incredible power to discuss. This power is displayed as we express gratitude and appreciation in our journey of manifesting the life we desire. When we place our trust in God, set our intentions, and take inspired action, we should express sincere gratitude and appreciation by showering our Creator with praise.

Constantly expressing gratitude transforms our perspective and fills our hearts with joy and contentment. This act of acknowledging and expressing deep appreciation for the blessings, big and small, that grace our lives is reciprocated When we cultivate an attitude of gratitude, we open ourselves to receive even more abundance and blessings from our loving Creator.

As we manifest the life we want, we should remember to pause and reflect on the countless gifts bestowed upon us. Every breath we take, every sunrise that paints the sky, every kind word spoken to us, and every opportunity that comes our way, are reasons to be overflowing with gratitude. When we acknowledge these blessings and offer thanks to God, we create a powerful ripple effect in our lives.

Expressing gratitude allows us to shift our focus from what we lack to what we have. Doing so reminds us that there is abundance in our journey is and that even in challenging times, blessings surround us. Gratitude opens our eyes to the miracles that unfold daily and helps us cultivate a deep sense of appreciation for the present moment.

When we show gratitude to our Creator, we acknowledge that every manifestation, every step forward, is a gift from His infinite wisdom and love. We recognize that we are co-creators, partnering with God to bring our desires into reality. Gratitude humbles us and reminds us that we are not in control, but rather, we are guided and supported by a divine force far greater than ourselves.

So, let us make expressing gratitude a daily practice. Take a moment each day to pause, reflect, and give thanks. Offer prayers of gratitude, speak words of appreciation, or write in a journal to capture the blessings that unfold in your life. Let your heart overflow with gratitude for the love, guidance, and abundance that God showers upon you.

But do not stop there. Let gratitude infuse every aspect of your life. Express appreciation to the people around you, who support and uplift you. Be grateful for the lessons learned from challenges and setbacks, for they are catalysts for growth. Demonstrate gratitude as a way of life and watch as it magnifies the beauty and blessings that flow into your being.

Remember, gratitude is not just a fleeting emotion but a transformative way of being. It connects us to the divine source of all creation and fills our souls with an overwhelming sense of awe and wonder. So, let us bow our hearts in humble gratitude, lift our voices in heartfelt appreciation, and celebrate the magnificent journey of manifesting the life we want with unending gratitude to our Creator.

Gratitude is the key that unlocks the doors to even greater abundance and fulfillment. Let your heart overflow with gratitude, for through it, you will continue to attract miracles, blessings, and a life beyond your greatest dreams.

Keep manifesting, keep trusting, and keep embracing gratitude, my friend. Your journey is blessed, and your appreciation is a beautiful melody that resonates with the heart of the Creator.

## Live in Abundance

Now is as good a time as any to realise the wondrous world of living in abundance! Picture this: a life filled with boundless joy, love, prosperity, and fulfillment. Can you feel the excitement tingling in your soul? Living in abundance is not just a dream; it is a tangible reality waiting to be experienced.

Living in abundance is about shifting our mindset from scarcity to a mindset of limitless possibilities. It is in recognizing that the universe is overflowing with blessings, and we are deserving of every single one. When we believe in our worthiness and open ourselves up to receive, we unlock the doors to a life filled with abundance in all its magnificent forms.

Abundance is not solely about material possessions or financial wealth, although they may be part of it. Rather, it involves recognizing and embracing the abundant beauty that surrounds us every day. It involves cultivating rich relationships, nurturing our physical and emotional well-being, and basking in the wonders of the present moment.

Living in abundance starts with expressing gratitude. When we appreciate the blessings, we already have, we create a fertile ground for more abundance to flow into our lives. Gratitude opens our hearts and shifts our focus from what is lacking to what is abundant and allowing us to celebrate the smallest joys and the grandest miracles, reminding us that we are truly blessed.

To live in abundance, we must release the limitations we impose upon ourselves. We must let go of self-doubt, fear, and the belief that we are not enough. Embrace your unique talents, passions, and dreams. Trust in your abilities and have faith that the universe supports in your favour. When you step into your authentic power, the world becomes your playground of possibilities.

Living in abundance beings by choosing thoughts and beliefs that align with abundance. Affirmations become your daily mantra, reinforcing your belief in your inherent abundance. Visualize the life you desire, feel the emotions of already having it, and watch as the universe responds to your unwavering faith.

Abundance is not a destination; it is a way of being that develops from our attitude of gratitude, a mindset of possibility, and a recognition of the unlimited potential within. Embrace the abundance that exists within and around you, as it guides your actions, decisions, and interactions with others.
But remember, living in abundance is not a solitary journey. On this journey, you must share the abundance with others, lifting them up, and celebrating their successes. This creates a ripple effect. impacting our world where everyone can experience abundance and prosper.

I urge you to open your arms wide and embrace the abundance that is waiting for you. Believe in the infinite possibilities that lie ahead. Celebrate the richness of life in every moment and watch as the universe responds to your unwavering faith. Living in abundance is your birthright, and now is the time to claim it with passion, purpose, and a grateful heart.

May your days be filled with abundance in every aspect of your existence, and may you radiate the light of abundance to inspire others on their own journey.

Embrace the magnificence of living in abundance and let your soul dance to the rhythm of a life truly lived to the fullest.

# Give Back to Others

There is a profound beauty in extending a helping hand, touching lives, and making a positive impact on the world around us. Such an experience fills our hearts with boundless joy, ignites our souls with purpose, and reminds us of the interconnectedness among humanity.

Giving back is not just an act of kindness; the expression encompasses love and compassion and recognizing that we have the power to have influence, no matter how big or small, in someone else's life. Let us perceive it as a testament to our humanity, a way of showing empathy and support to those who may be facing challenges or in need of a helping hand.

When we give back, we open ourselves up to a world of fulfillment and abundance, and highlighting the paradoxical truth that the more we give, the more we receive. It is not about seeking recognition or rewards; it is about the intrinsic joy that comes from selflessly giving without expecting anything in return.

Giving back takes many forms. It could be volunteering your time and skills for a cause you deeply care about, lending a listening ear to someone facing despair, or sharing your knowledge and experiences to inspire others.

Do no doubt that it may be as simple as a warm smile, a kind word, or a random act of kindness that brightens someone's day.

When we give back, we could be wittingly paying it forward, which creates a ripple effect of positivity. Each act of giving has the power to spark transformation, not only in the lives of others but also within us.

Giving back is an opportunity to connect with our shared humanity, it reminds us that we are all interconnected, that we are part of something greater than ourselves. That selfless act breaks down barriers, transcends differences, and unites us in the universal language of love and compassion.

But there is a bonus to giving back! when we give, we receive so much more in return. We receive a sense of purpose and fulfillment that cannot be measured. We witness the impact of our actions, the smiles we bring, and the lives we touch. We experience a deep gratitude for the blessings in our own lives, and we realize the immense power we hold to make a positive difference.

Let us embrace the transformative power of giving back by extend our hearts and hands to those in need. Let us share our love, our resources, and our time with others. In doing so, we create a world where compassion reigns, where kindness knows no bounds, and where each person can give back.

Together, we will create a legacy of love and of generosity by being the change we wish to see in the world. As wee give back with all our hearts, we light up the world with compassion and make it a brighter, more beautiful place for all.

Banding together let us embark on this beautiful journey of giving back and let our souls dance in the symphony of selflessness. Together, we can be effective, one act of kindness at a time.

# Let Glow

Let Glow! You can enhance your personal growth journey. Are you ready to embrace your authentic self, shine bright, and make a positive impact on your world?

Let Glow is the ultimate culmination of our personal growth journey. It is a momentous accomplishment when we have learned to love ourselves unconditionally, set healthy boundaries, and live a life of abundance. We have released those limiting beliefs that held us back for so long, and now are ready to embrace our true selves and let our inner light shine.

But what does it mean to Let Glow? At its essence, let glow is all about being true to who we are, living mindfully, and spreading love and positivity to those around us. It starts with releasing all those negative thoughts and emotions that weigh us down. We forgive ourselves and others, and we open our hearts to change and growth.

When we Let Glow, we transmit energy. It is like a beacon of light that radiates outwards, touching the lives of those we encounter. We inspire others to embrace their own authenticity and live their best lives.

So, how do we Let Glow? Here are some actions to implement in our daily lives that got me started.

First, practice self-awareness. Take the time to reflect on your values, beliefs, and goals. Understand what truly drives you and what makes you uniquely you. Embrace both your strengths and weaknesses, celebrating your achievements while also acknowledging areas for growth.

Second, be true to yourself. Do not shape yourself into someone else's idea of who you should be. Embrace your authentic self and let your true colours shine through. Speak your truth, express your thoughts and feelings, and stand up for what you believe in.

Third, unleash your creativity! Explore your artistic side and find joy in self-expression. Whether it is through art, music, writing, or any other form of creative outlet, let your inner artist shine and share your uniqueness with the world.
Fourth, surround yourself with positive influences. Connect with people who uplift and support you. Spend time with those who share your values and passions. Build a tribe of like-minded individuals who inspire and encourage you on your journey.

Fifth, remember to practice self-care. Take care of your physical, mental, emotional, and spiritual well-being. Prioritize activities that nourish your soul and make you feel good. Whether it is taking a walk-in nature, indulging in a bubble bath, or practicing mindfulness and meditation, make self-care a non-negotiable part of your routine.

And remember that Let Glow is a journey, not a destination. Embrace the process and enjoy every step along the way. Allow yourself to grow, evolve, and learn. Each day brings new opportunities to let your light shine even brighter.

Let go and LETGLOW... You got this!

Embrace your authenticity, practice mindfulness, and let your positive energy light up the world. When we do this, we create a ripple effect of love, joy, and transformation. Let us make every moment count and live a life that truly glows with passion and purpose!

# Conclusion

In the depths of our souls there is the potential for an extraordinary transformation. The journey towards self-love, self-acceptance, and personal growth may be filled with challenges, but the rewards are immeasurable. It is an odyssey that demands our courage, vulnerability, and unwavering determination.

As we embark on this sacred expedition, we must be willing to confront the shadows that linger within us. It is in releasing the heavy burdens of self-doubt, fear, and negativity that we can truly soar. Let Glow- compels us to shed the layers that no longer serve us, liberating ourselves from the shackles that hold us back.

Embrace your authenticity, for within it lies the power to ignite your spirit. Embrace the unique qualities that set you apart, for that is the key to unlocking your true potential. In a world that often tries to form us into something we are not, let us have the audacity to be ourselves, unapologetically.

With a heart full of gratitude and a mind focused on positivity, we can cultivate a mindset that attracts abundance and joy. Nurture your soul with self-care, for it is through tending to our own needs that we have the strength to lift others. Surround yourself with those who uplift you, who see the brilliance within you, and who inspire you to reach higher.

But remember, that this journey is not solely for our own benefit. It is also an opportunity to give back, to touch the lives of others with love and compassion. In the act of extending a helping hand, we discover the true essence of our humanity. By nurturing relationships, showing kindness, and making a difference, we create a ripple effect of positivity that can transform lives and uplift the world.

Let your light shine, for within you lie a radiance that is meant to illuminate the darkness. Embrace the challenges and setbacks as steppingstones towards growth. Embrace the triumphs and victories as reminders of your resilience and strength. Your journey towards Letting Glow is a testament to your courage and determination.

So, as you continue along this path, always remember to prioritize self-care, set boundaries that honour your worth, and practice gratitude for the blessings that surround you. Embrace the beautiful soul that you are and let your light shine brightly for all to see.

You have the power to create a life of purpose, joy, and fulfillment. Embrace your journey, embrace your authentic self, and embrace the incredible person you are becoming. Let your light radiate, inspire, and transform. Let Glow and watch as the world is forever changed by the brilliance of your spirit.

Made in the USA
Columbia, SC
29 January 2024

30617009R00059